CACHE

D0416517

Penny Tassoni

CARING FOR CHILDREN

www.pearsonschoolsandfe.co.uk

✓ Free online support
✓ Useful weblinks
✓ 24 hour online ordering

0845 630 44 44

Part of Pearson

Heinemann is an imprint of Pearson Education Limited, Edinburgh Gate, Harlow, Essex, CM20 2JE.

www.pearsonschoolsandfecolleges.co.uk

Heinemann is a registered trademark of Pearson Education Limited

Text © Penny Tassoni, 2011
Designed by Sam Charrington
Layouts by Lorraine Inglis Design
Original illustrations © Pearson Education Limited 2011
Illustrated by Oxford Designers & Illustrators Ltd and Lorraine Inglis Design
Cover design by Sam Charrington
Picture research by Harriet Merry
Cover photo © Getty Images: Reggie Casagrande

The rights of Penny Tassoni to be identified as author of this work have been asserted by her
in accordance with the Copyright, Designs and Patents Act 1988.

First published 2011

14 13 12 11
10 9 8 7 6 5 4 3 2

British Library Cataloguing in Publication Data
A catalogue record for this book is available from the British Library

ISBN 978 0 435 04754 2

Printed in Spain by Grafos S.A.

Acknowledgements
The author and publisher would like to thank the following individuals and organisations for permission to reproduce logos and photographs:

p76: Lion Mark reproduced with permission of the British Toy & Hobby Association

Photographs
(Key: b-bottom; c-centre; l-left; r-right; t-top)
Alamy Images: Adrian Sherratt 92, Peter Arnold Inc. 157, Bubbles Photolibrary 16, 115, Coyote-Photography.co.uk 146tr, Olaf Doering 179, Flonline digitale Bildagentur GmbH 102tr, Sally and Richard Greenhill 170, Johnny Greig LSL 146, Jacky Chapman 162bl, Jaubert Images 225, Beau Lark / Fancy 105, moodboard 218, Picture Contact BV 108br, PV Stock 131b, tbkmedia.de 95tr, TMO Pictures 162, Ian West 182c, Westend61 GmbH 166; Bananastock: alamy 129, Imagestate 133, 152, 162tr, 200, 206; Corbis: Laura Dwight 158, Jose Luis Pelaez, Inc. 108bl, Ocean 142, Craig Pulsifer / Aurora Open 184, Radius Images 115br, Tetra Images 108; Getty Images: Andy Andrews 131, Axiom Photographic Agency 95tl, Blend Images 115tr, Paul Bradbury 8, Joe Cornish 29, Peter Dazeley 104, Ty Downing / Workbook Stock 91, Fuse 156, Robert Glenn / DK Stock 153, Steve Gorten / Dorling Kindersly 135, Ian Hooten / SPL 196, Meridith Hoyer / Stockbyte 95, Anthony Lee / OJO Images 19, Jose Luis Pelaez Inc / Blend Images 177, Howard Shooter 99, Chris Stein 18, Susan Barr 84, 96, Nicola Sutton / Life File 182, Tooga 159; Imagestate Media: Bananastock 23, 26bl, 89, Kevin Peterson 35cl; Pearson Education Ltd: Gareth Boden 59r, 102bl, 102br, 181, 223, Chris Parker 42, vi, Creatas 114, 115tl, Jules Selmes 13, 21, 40c, 66, 110, 117, 119, 122, 123tr, 123cl, 125, 131l, 134, 140, 146bl, 147br, 149, 154, 155, 162br, 169, 173b, 176, Lisa Payne Photography 22, 93, Lord and Leverett 11, 26br, 38, 40br, Anna Marlow 165, Mind Studio 50, Kevin Petersen 40tr, Richard Smith 189, Studio 8 15, 24, 27br, 35c, 107, 108tr, 112, 150, 173, 173t, 174, 175, Tudor Photography 26, 35cr, 102, Roddy Paine 13/1, 13/3, 13/4, 13/5, 13/6, 27, 28l, 28r, 116, 116b, 120t, 120r, 120b, 123, 136, 137, 138; PhotoDisc: Photodisk 147tr; Rex Features: 146br, JIM PICKERELL 161; Shutterstock.com: Aaron Amat 47l, Yuri Arcurs 207, auremar 41b, Blue Orange Studio 98, Greenland 175t, Anton Gvozdikov 41t, GW Images 36, Jorg Hackemann 40bl, Hannamariah 49c, Margo Harrison 147, Hitdelight 59b, Ian Wilson 127, Kzenon 219, Robyn Mackenzie 194, Marjanneke de Jong 147bl, Monkey Business Images 32, 33, Nils 7 47b, Renata Osinska 182b, Losevsky Pavel 83, 173cl, Norman Pogson 37, Glenda M. Powers 40tl, Ruta Saulyte-Laurinaviciene 123cr, Tomasz Trojanowski 27c, Tompet 26cr, Sergey Toronto 95br, vovan 47tr, Voyagerix 123b, Duzan Zidar 49l. All other images © Pearson Education

Every effort has been made to contact copyright holders of material reproduced in this book. Any omissions will be rectified in subsequent printings if notice is given to the publishers. We apologise in advance for any unintentional omissions.

Websites
There are links to relevant websites in this book. In order to ensure that the links are up to date and that the links work we have made the links available on our website at www.pearsonhotlinks.co.uk. Search for this title, CACHE Entry Level 3/Level 1 Caring for Children Student Book or ISBN 9780435047542.

Contents

Who is this book for?

This book has been written to support the CACHE Entry Level 3 Award and Certificate in Caring for a Child/Children and the Level I Award, Certificate and Diploma in Caring for Children. Although these courses do not qualify you to work with children they do help you prepare for your next steps – whether you want to continue in training or go into the world of work. They will also give you the opportunity to develop valuable life skills.

Features of this book

- This book has 10 **chapters** and covers a total of 22 **units**.
- Each chapter has units which exactly match the units of the CACHE qualification.
- Each unit is split into learning topics which explain everything you need to know.
- The information on each page is clear and easy to find.
- The first page of each chapter tells you which units are covered and what you are going to learn about.

 You can read about all the features of this book on the page opposite.

A note from the author

Working with children can be hard work but very interesting. You need a lot of patience but also knowledge. This is why it takes time to become qualified. By taking the Entry Level 3 or Level I Caring for Children course you have started out on this journey. I hope that this book will help you on your way.

Penny Tassoni

High Five! gives you 5 important things you need to know.

Entry Level 3 units and Level 1 units are shown in different colours so you can spot the units which are for you.

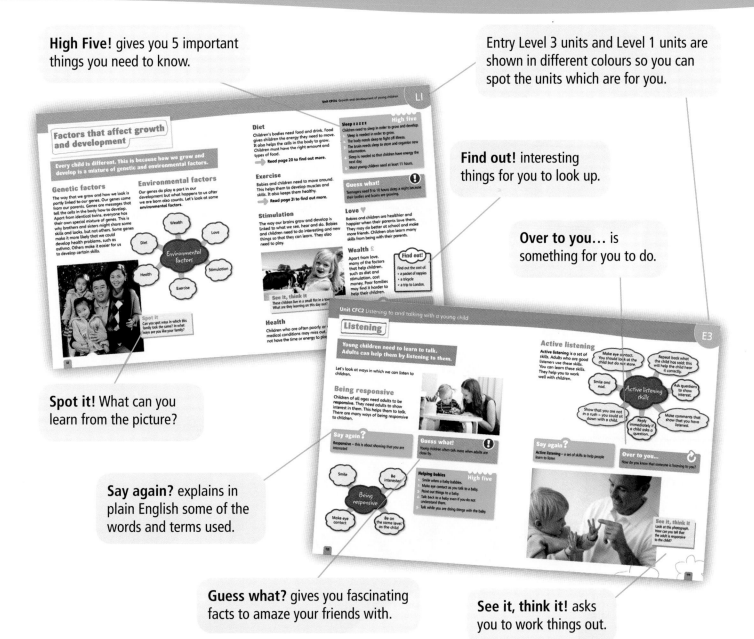

Find out! interesting things for you to look up.

Over to you... is something for you to do.

Spot it! What can you learn from the picture?

Say again? explains in plain English some of the words and terms used.

Guess what? gives you fascinating facts to amaze your friends with.

See it, think it! asks you to work things out.

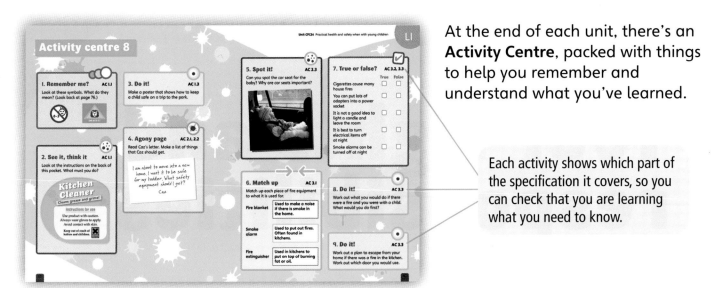

At the end of each unit, there's an **Activity Centre**, packed with things to help you remember and understand what you've learned.

Each activity shows which part of the specification it covers, so you can check that you are learning what you need to know.

1

Your rights and responsibilities

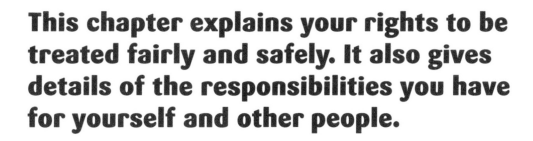

This chapter explains your rights to be treated fairly and safely. It also gives details of the responsibilities you have for yourself and other people.

The unit covered in this chapter is:

IRRE3 Individual rights and responsibilities

In this chapter you will learn about:

- your right to be treated fairly when shopping, at work and in housing
- your rights to keep you safe at work
- your rights to privacy
- where you can find sources of support
- your responsibilities to keep yourself healthy and safe
- your responsibility to work hard
- your responsibilities towards others, respect others' feelings, property and safety.

Your rights

Everyone has rights. Some rights are about the way people can treat you. Other rights are about what you are allowed to do.

There are many rules and laws to protect your rights. These laws are often called human rights. Let's look at some.

Right to be treated fairly

There are laws to make sure that you are treated fairly. These were made because some groups of people were not always treated fairly.

I did not get a job because I am a girl. The company got into trouble.

My boss kept on touching me. I didn't like it. She got into trouble.

Shopping

You have rights when you shop.

I got my money back because the watch did not work.

Work

Employers have to treat you fairly.

Spot it

Can you spot how this shop helps people in wheelchairs to be treated fairly?

Guess what!

Many of our rights come under the Human Rights Act.

Rights to keep you safe

There are laws to keep you safe.

Work

Your employer must keep you safe when you are at work.

> My boss gives us gloves and an apron when changing nappies.

Rights of privacy

You have some rights to privacy.

> School had to ask before putting photographs of me in the newspaper.

Housing

Landlords have to make sure that things are safe for you.

> There was a smell of gas in my flat. My landlord had to make it safe.

> Doctors and teachers cannot gossip about me.

Find out!

Can you think of a right that you have?

Sources of support

It is good to know where you can get help.
You should not have to pay to get help.

Trades Union Congress
They help people who are in work. You can get advice about your rights.

Equality and Human Rights Commission
They give advice and information when people have not been treated fairly.

Support and information

Citizens Advice Bureau
You will find them in most towns. They give free information and advice.

Health and Safety Executive
They sort out health and safety. You can get advice and information.

Consumer Direct
They give advice and help about things that you have bought or are using.

 To obtain a secure link to the websites of the support and information organisations, see the Website section on page ii.

Responsibilities

As well as rights, you also have responsibilities. This is because we have to take care of ourselves and respect other people.

Let's look at what **responsibilities** you have.

Say again?

Responsibility – something that you have to do/say

Staying healthy

You have a right to medical care. But you have a responsibility to stay healthy.

- Eat five portions of fruit and vegetables a day.
- Cut down on sugary and fatty snacks.
- Take some exercise.
- Wear condoms if you have sex.
- Do not smoke.

Staying safe

You have some rights to be kept safe at work, in the street and at home, but you have to keep yourself safe.

- Be careful when crossing the road.
- Follow instructions on labels.
- Wear a cycle helmet.
- Be careful when using tools or knives.

Spot it
Can you spot who is working hard?

Working hard

You have a right to education, but you have a responsibility to work hard.

- Listen to your teacher.
- Turn phones off.
- Do not listen to music.
- Do your homework.

Your responsibilities   **High five**

1. Work hard.
2. Eat healthy foods.
3. Keep fit.
4. Keep clean.
5. Keep safe.

Responsibilities towards others

You have rights about the way people treat you. Here are some of the responsibilities that you have towards others.

Respect others' feelings

You have a responsibility to respect other people.

- Be polite and kind.
- Take your turn in a queue.
- Don't swear in public.
- Don't say unkind things about others.
- Don't bully others.
- Don't gossip about people.

Respect property

People have a right to property and belongings.

- Do not steal other people's things.
- Do not damage other people's things.
- Do not write on walls.
- Do not drop litter.

Safety

You have a responsibility not to hurt others.

- Do not drive badly.
- Do not play with fireworks.
- Follow safety instructions.
- Use a condom if you have sex.

See it, think it
How are the people in this street being responsible? Does it seem a happy place?

Activity centre 1

1. Remember me? AC 1.1

Why are Human Rights important?
Name one right that is important
for you.

4. Over to you... AC 1.1

Have you ever been treated unfairly?
What did it feel like?

2. Do it! AC 1.2

Go to the Equality and Human Rights
Commission website. Why could they
help someone who has not been
treated fairly?

To obtain a secure link to the website
see the Websites section on page ii.

5. Agony page AC 1.2

Read Jodie's letter. Is this fair? Who
could Jodie talk to about this?

> I went for a job as a plumber.
> They told me that I could not
> have it. They told me it was
> because I was a girl.
>
> Jodie

3. Odd one out! AC 1.1

Which one of these is not a right?

To be safe at work

**For personal information to be kept
private**

To be given lots of money

To be treated fairly when at work

6. True or false?　AC 1.3, 1.4

Which two of these are not true?

	True	False
You must take care of yourself	☐	☐
You can bully other people	☐	☐
You can call people names	☐	☐
You should do your best at school or college	☐	☐

7. Case study　AC 1.2

C

My name is Jo. I am black. I also have sight problems. When I went for a job in an office, I did not get it. They said it was because I would not fit in. It was not fair. I knew that I could do the work. I went to the Citizens' Advice Bureau. They were great. They made lots of calls and wrote lots of letters for me. After a few weeks, I was told that I could have the job in the office. Now I am there, I work very hard. My boss is happy.

1. Why was Jo not being treated fairly?
2. Where did Jo go to get help?
3. What responsibility does Jo have now?

2

Human growth and development

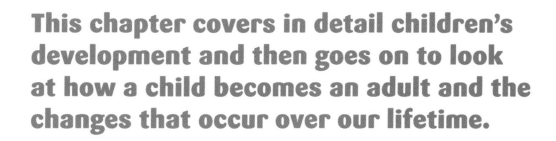

This chapter covers in detail children's development and then goes on to look at how a child becomes an adult and the changes that occur over our lifetime.

The units covered in this chapter are:

CFC 14 Growth and development of young children
CFC 15 Human growth and development

In this chapter you will learn about:

- the patterns and stages of growth for children from birth to 5 years 11 months
- factors which influence growth and development from birth to 5 years 11 months
- the importance of diet and exercise for children's growth and development
- activities which promote children's physical development
- ways to help children to develop communication and language skills and ways to encourage children to play socially
- the main stages of growth and development across the human lifespan
- what is meant by physical, intellectual, emotional and social development
- factors which may affect physical growth and development
- circumstances or life events which may affect an individual's emotional and social well-being
- the effects of ageing in the later stages of life.

Patterns and stages of growth

Babies and children grow and develop. Adults who work with them need to know how to help them and also what to expect.

Over the next few pages, we will look at what most children can do at different ages.

But there are four main points about **growth** and **development** to look at first.

1. Children's body shape changes

As children grow, their body shape changes. Babies have a large head compared with the rest of their body.

2. Development follows a sequence

The way that children learn to do things follows a sequence. Babies sit before they walk. They babble before they talk.

Say again?

Growth – this is about how children's bodies get taller and heavier
Development – this is about the way children learn to use their bodies and gain skills

3. Development can be put into areas

To help look at children's development it is put into areas. But many skills rely on development in more than one area. The spider diagram opposite shows these areas.

Guess what!

The rate of development varies between children.

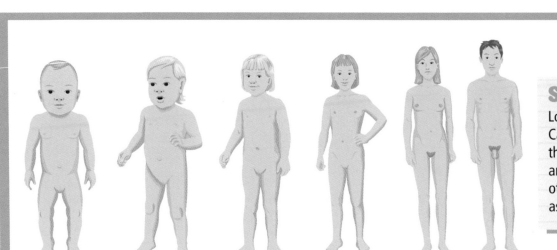

Spot it
Look at the pictures. Can you spot how the trunk, legs and arms make up more of children's bodies as they get older?

Physical
Being able to use the body,
e.g. walking, picking up toys

Cognitive/intellectual
Being able to think and learn,
e.g. remember things, read

Areas of development

Emotional
Being able to care about
others and control feelings
such as anger

Communication and language
Being able to talk, listen and
understand others

Social
Being able to live, play and
work with others

See it, think it
What skills are these
children learning?

4. Development is measured using milestones

Adults who work with children look out for
particular skills at different ages. These are
often called **milestones**. Children who are
not meeting the milestones for their age
sometimes need help.

Say again?

Milestones – these are certain skills that most
children reach at a certain age

Babies: the first year!

Babies change quickly in their first year. They grow fast and develop many skills. By their first birthday they can feed themselves, understand many words and move about.

Physical development

Babies are born with some key reflexes. These keep them alive. They can cry, suck and grasp objects.

Age	Stage of development	How to help
Newborn	• Reflexes – crying, sucking and grasping. • Cries to get help.	• Plenty of cuddles. • Talk and gently rock. • Respond to cries.
6 weeks	• Smiles and coos. • Watches parents' or carer's faces when held. • Has different cries when tired or hungry.	• Let them kick without a nappy. • Talk and smile to them. • Shake rattles gently.
3 months	• Starts to lift head. • Can hold a rattle.	• Hold and talk to them. • Sing nursery rhymes. • Give them safe objects to hold.
6 months	• Enjoys sitting on adult's lap. • Babbles. • Can pass toys from hand to hand. • Starts weaning.	• Look at books together. • Talk back when they babble. • Put out stacking beakers so they can knock them down.
9 months	• Sits up alone. • May be crawling or shuffling. • Understands some words. • Can pick up small objects.	• Play action games such as 'Humpty Dumpty'. • Put out safe objects and toys for them to play with on the floor.
12 months	• May be standing up by holding on to furniture. • Drinks from a cup. • Self feeds with finger foods such as toast. • Points to things.	• Show picture books. • Take an interest in what they are pointing to. • Sing rhymes. • Talk, but allow time for them to babble back.

Cognitive development

Babies' brains grow very quickly in their first year. This allows them to progress in all areas of development. Babies also learn quickly. They remember important people. They repeat things that they enjoy, for example, shaking a rattle. They also learn to look for things that are hidden in front of them.

Say again?

Cognitive development – this is about the way children think, learn and remember things

Communication and language development

Babies begin by crying, but quickly start to make other sounds. By the age of 6 months, most babies are babbling. This is the start of their talking. By 10 months, most babies know a few words, but they cannot talk yet.

Social and emotional development

Babies quickly recognise key people in their lives. They start to look for them and trust them. By 8 months babies start to cry if their parent or carer goes out of sight. In this year, they also learn to play with their parents or carers. They play 'peepo' or knock down stacking beakers.

What babies need   High five

1. Babies need a lot of time with parents and carers.
2. Babies need to be cuddled and smiled at.
3. Babies need to hear people talking to them.
4. Babies do best with breast milk.
5. Babies need parents and carers to play with them.

Toddlers 1-3 years

Toddlers are busy little people who enjoy exploring and moving around. It can be hard work to look after a toddler.

During this stage of their lives, **toddlers** will learn many skills that will help them. Let's look at how quickly they change.

Say again ?

Toddler – the word for children from the time they start to walk until around 3 years old

Special things about toddlers   High five

1. Toddlers find it hard to wait.
2. Toddlers like to do things for themselves.
3. When toddlers get tired or fed up, they often fly into a rage.
4. Sharing is hard for toddlers.
5. Toddlers like to copy what adults are doing.

Age	Stage of development
At 18 months	<ul><li>can say 15 words</li><li>point out objects to their carers</li><li>can pull off their shoes</li><li>can roll and throw a ball</li><li>can walk downstairs with an adult</li><li>cry when left with people they do not know</li></ul>
At 2 years	<ul><li>put two words together to make a mini-sentence – e.g. 'cat gone'</li><li>use a spoon to feed themselves</li><li>can build a tower of five bricks</li><li>play alongside other children</li><li>want to be independent</li><li>do not understand why they have to wait or cannot have things</li><li>cry when left with people they do not know</li></ul>
At 3 years	<ul><li>can talk quite well and use questions</li><li>can walk and run confidently</li><li>draw a face</li><li>can put on and take off their coat</li><li>play with other children</li><li>are out of nappies</li><li>can be left with people they do not know for short periods of time</li><li>can build a tower of nine or ten bricks</li></ul>

See it, think it
Look at the skills in the table above. Can you work out which areas of development these skills link to?

Toddler play

There are some things that most toddlers love to do. Once they have found something that they like to do, they will often do it over and over again.

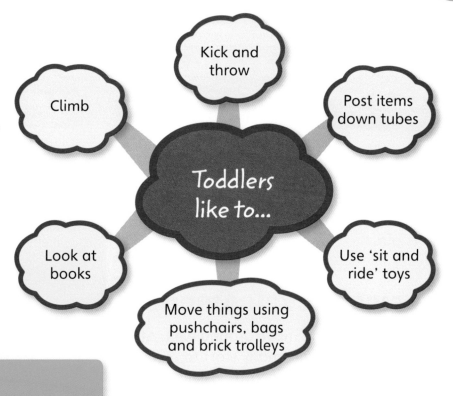

Kick and throw

Climb

Post items down tubes

Toddlers like to...

Use 'sit and ride' toys

Look at books

Move things using pushchairs, bags and brick trolleys

Say again ?

Transporting – this is about the way that toddlers love moving things from place to place

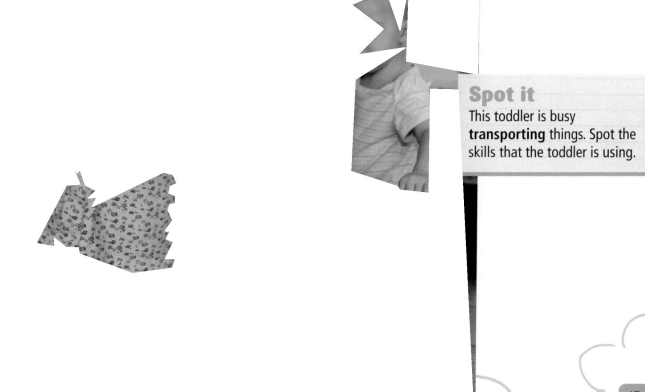

Spot it
This toddler is busy **transporting** things. Spot the skills that the toddler is using.

Children from 3 to 6 years

While babies and toddlers grow and develop quickly, children at 3, 4 and 5 years grow and develop at a slower pace.

Between the ages of 3 and 6 years, children will perfect many skills and learn new ones. There will be some big changes for them too. Most children will start school at 4 or 5 years old.

Physical development

Children can run and move around well. At the age of 4 or 5 years, many start to enjoy using bicycles and learning other skills such as swimming. Smaller hand movements are also developing well. Children can usually cut with scissors at 4 years and can make marks with crayons and pencils. These skills are needed for handwriting.

Communication and language development

By the age of 4 years, children should be talking well. They make some odd mistakes, for example, saying 'swimmed' or 'tooked', but this is normal. Most children can also recognise their name by 4 years and will go on to write it. By 6 years, most children can read some simple books although they may need help.

See it, think it
This child is about to start school. It is a long time since she was a baby. Make a list of skills that she has gained.

Cognitive development

Children's learning really takes off when they are about 3 years old. They start to ask questions and remember things easily. By 4 years, most children know a few colours and may start to count. By the age of 6 years, most children can play simple games such as 'snap' and 'pairs'.

Emotional development

Children's behaviour becomes more settled from the age of 3 years onwards. This is linked to their language. They can understand what is being said. They can also tell us what it is they want. This makes them happier. Children also start to be more confident. They find it easier to cope when they cannot be with their parents for a few hours.

Social development

Children love playing with other children now. They have the skills to share and take turns. They can also talk and listen to each other. Having friends becomes very important.

Play and learning

Children in this age group will do most of their learning through play. Let's look at what they might enjoy doing.

Dressing up

Climbing frames

Sand, dough and water

Children aged 3 to 6 like...

Painting and drawing

Trains, cars and pretend animals

Puzzles and bricks

Factors that affect growth and development

Every child is different. This is because how we grow and develop is a mixture of genetic and environmental factors.

Genetic factors

The way that we grow and how we look is partly linked to our genes. Our genes come from our parents. Genes are messages that tell the cells in the body how to develop. Apart from identical twins, everyone has their own special mixture of genes. This is why brothers and sisters might share some skills and looks, but not others. Some genes make it more likely that we could develop health problems, such as asthma. Others make it easier for us to develop certain skills.

Environmental factors

Our genes do play a part in our development but what happens to us after we are born also counts. Let's look at some **environmental factors**.

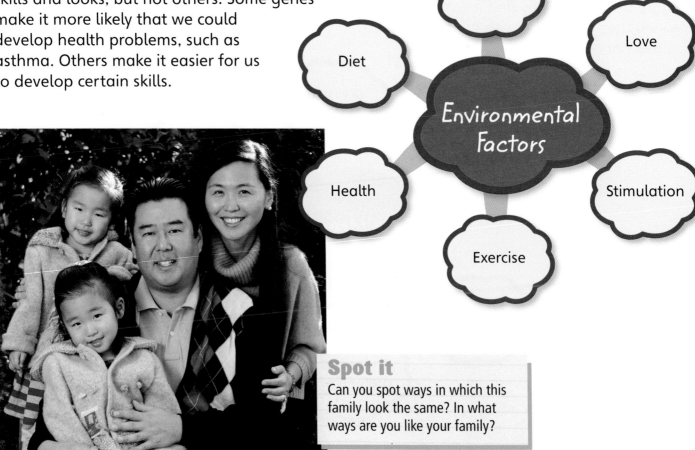

Wealth

Love

Diet

Environmental Factors

Stimulation

Health

Exercise

Spot it

Can you spot ways in which this family look the same? In what ways are you like your family?

Diet

Children's bodies need food and drink. Food gives children the energy they need to move. It also helps the cells in the body to grow. Children must have the right amount and types of food.

 Read page 20 to find out more.

Exercise

Babies and children need to move around. This helps them to develop muscles and skills. It also keeps them healthy.

 Read page 21 to find out more.

Stimulation

The way our brains grow and develop is linked to what we see, hear and do. Babies and children need to do interesting and new things so that they can learn. They also need to play.

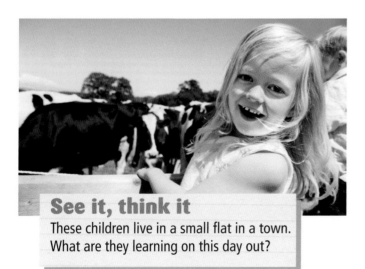

See it, think it
These children live in a small flat in a town. What are they learning on this day out?

Health

Children who are often poorly or who have medical conditions may miss out. They may not have the time or energy to play or exercise.

Sleep z z z z z — High five

Children need to sleep in order to grow and develop.

1. Sleep is needed in order to grow.
2. The body needs sleep to fight off illness.
3. The brain needs sleep to store and organise new information.
4. Sleep is needed so that children have energy the next day.
5. Most young children need at least 11 hours.

Guess what!

Teenagers need 9 to 10 hours sleep a night because their bodies and brains are growing.

Love ♥

Babies and children are healthier and happier when their parents love them. They may do better at school and make more friends. Children also learn many skills from being with their parents.

Wealth £

Apart from love, many of the factors that help children, such as diet and stimulation, cost money. Poor families may find it harder to help their children.

Find out!

Find out the cost of:
- a packet of nappies
- a tricycle
- a trip to London.

Say again

Genetic – the things that you inherit from your parents, including the way you look and some medical conditions
Environmental factors – the things that have happened to you in your life, e.g. going to school

The importance of diet and exercise

Children need the right amount of food and the right amount of exercise in order to grow and develop well.

Diet

A healthy diet is about giving children the right types of food and drink for their age. The spider diagram shows four ways in which a healthy diet helps babies and children.

Different ages need different diets

Giving children a healthy diet means making sure they are getting the right foods for their age. A baby will have only breast or formula milk for the first 6 months, but at I year will be having some milk and some meals. Children must also be given the right quantity of food. Too much food, even if it is healthy is stored by the body as fat. This can make it harder for children to play and move around.

 Read more about healthy foods on pages 44–46 and 48.

Gives children energy to move around

Helps the body to fight infection

A healthy diet...

Gives children energy to concentrate and learn

Helps children to grow in height and strength

Guess what!

The energy in food is measured in kilocalories (calories).

Spot it
Look at these plates. Spot the plate for the baby, the toddler and the 4 year old.

Exercise

Exercise is about moving around. Babies and young children exercise when they are playing. This might be crawling to get a toy or running around outdoors.

Spot it
These children are playing, but they are also taking exercise. Can you spot the skills that they are using?

Exercise   High five

1. Exercise is needed to develop muscles.
2. Exercise helps children to sleep better.
3. Exercise makes bones stronger.
4. Exercise helps children to learn skills.
5. Exercise makes children feel good.

Guess what!

The heart is a muscle. It gets stronger when you exercise.

Activities to promote physical development

Adults working with children often plan activities to help with children's physical development. There are many different physical skills that children need to develop. Let's look at them.

Physical skills

Activities for children have to be fun. They also have to help different physical skills.

Fine motor skills

Gross motor skills

Physical skills

Balance and co-ordination

Strength and stamina

Fine motor skills

These are hand skills.

Gross motor skills

These are movements made with arms and legs.

Balance and co-ordination

These help children to move easily.

Strength and stamina

These help children to stay healthy and develop.

Different skills come together

We have seen that children need different physical skills. Most of the time, children will use more than one skill at once. A child may walk and hold a ball at the same time. When you plan physical activities for children, try to think about how many skills they will be using.

See it, think it

Many activities will involve more than one type of skill. Look at this photograph and think about which skills are being developed.

Different activities for different ages

It is important that activities are right for the age and stage of children. If an activity is too hard for children, they will not enjoy it. If an activity is too easy, they will become bored. Below are some examples of activities that you could try with children.

Role of adults

High five

1. Work out what a child can already do.
2. Plan a fun activity to develop a skill further.
3. Check that equipment is safe.
4. Encourage the child to join in.
5. Praise the child's efforts.

Age/Stage	Gross motor; balance and co-ordination	Fine motor
Non-mobile babies	Play Humpty Dumpty and other action rhymes.	Encourage baby to hold and shake rattle.
Mobile babies (can crawl or move)	Make a tower of stacking beakers for them to knock down.	Put out 'pop-up' toys. Put out everyday objects to explore such as spoons or saucepans.
Toddlers (can walk)	Put out sit-and-ride toys. Play with a large ball.	Play with shape sorters. Put out water and spoons.
Children from 3 years (can run and climb)	Put out wheeled toys, such as scooters. Play games with balls. Go for walks in the park.	Play with sand and dough. Put out crayons, pencils and paints.

Over to you...

For each age group in the table above, think of one more physical activity.

Spot it

Spot how many different physical activities these children are doing.

Guess what!

At 2½ years, most children will either be right or left handed.

Helping children with communication, language and play

Babies and children rely on adults to learn how to communicate and speak. There are some important ways in which we can help.

Ways to help babies

Babies need a lot of **interaction**. They need adults to hold them and make eye contact with them. They need adults to talk to them and point things out. Adults can show babies different things in the room, outside or in a picture book. Adults have to use their faces to show excitement and interest.

Say again ?

Interaction – making eye contact, listening as well as talking

Guess what!

Stuttering is common among children aged between 2 and 4 years.

Ways to help toddlers

Toddlers need adults to be very patient. They often know a few words, but find it hard to say them quickly. Their speech may not be clear until they are 3 years old. This makes it hard for them to communicate. Adults can help by giving toddlers time to think and answer. Toddlers can learn words quickly if adults talk to them and show them interesting things. Toddlers love books, songs and rhymes.

Working with toddlers and young children   High five

1. Get down to children's level and make eye contact.
2. Smile when you talk.
3. Use gestures and point to things.
4. Give children time to reply.
5. Be interested in what children say.

Spot it
This adult is helping a baby to learn language. Can you spot some skills that the adult is using?

Ways to help children 3–6 years

Adults can help children from 3 years by putting out play activities. Children can play in the home corner or work together to build a train set. Adults should try and play with children. Children learn new words when they see and do new things and so adults might bring in a puppet or take them out for a walk to the shops.

Guess what!

When children make a mistake when talking, adults need to say it back correctly.

So a 4 year old might say 'Last night I go to my gran's.'

The adult replies 'So you WENT to your gran's, did you?'

Ways to encourage children to play socially

It takes time for children to learn how to play with others. Most children will start doing this when they are about 3 years old.

Children need to learn about:

- taking turns
- listening to others
- understanding others
- sharing resources
- being part of a team
- sticking to the rules.

Babies

Babies do not play with other children, but adults can help them to enjoy play. Games for babies are quite simple. Many of them are action rhymes such as singing 'Row, row, row the boat' or 'Round and round the garden like a teddy bear'.

Toddlers

Toddlers start to be interested in playing with others. They are not good at following rules. They also do not understand about sharing. This means that adults have to work with them. Adults can make sure that everyone gets something to do. Toddlers love simple games which allow them to do things. They like chasing bubbles. They like pouring water out of containers.

Ways to help children from 3 until 6 years old

Most children from 3 years have enough language to help them play with others. They still need a little help from adults as they may squabble at times. Adults can help children by teaching them simple games. Many children like playing board games. Children also can make up games outside using balls, hoops and cones.

Top tips

- Make sure there is enough to play with.
- Keep an eye on children as they play.
- Model how to play nicely and take turns.

Activity centre 2

1. Match up
AC 1.1

Match the sentences to the photographs.

I like playing with my friends.

I only drink milk.

I can write my name.

I have just learned to walk.

I use the potty now.

Sudden noises make my arms and legs shoot out.

I have tantrums when I am frustrated.

I can say a few words now.

2. Do it!
AC 1.1

Make a poster that helps parents to know what children can do at different ages.

Try and find some pictures to put on it.

3. True or false?
AC 1.1

	True	False
At 3 years most children can read.	☐	☐
Babies can sit up alone by 9 months.	☐	☐
4 year olds like to play together.	☐	☐
Toddlers like to stay near their carers.	☐	☐
Babies can talk at 6 months.	☐	☐
2 year olds can share toys.	☐	☐

4. Remember me? AC I.2

Can you think of four factors that make a difference to the way children grow and develop? Look back at page 19 for more information.

5. Agony page AC I.3

Read the letter below. Can you tell these parents why exercise and diet is important?

HELP!

Our son is four years old. He spends a lot of time watching TV. He has a computer as well. He cries unless I give him sweets and crisps. I have been told that he needs a better diet and more exercise. I cannot see what the fuss is about.

6. Do it! AC 2.1

Make a poster showing four different physical activities for babies and young children.

7. Odd one out! AC 2.2

All but one of these activities will help children's language. Which is the odd one out?

Sharing books
Singing rhymes
Kicking a ball

8. Spot it! AC 2.3

Look at these photographs. Explain how children are learning to play socially in each one.

The main stages of human growth and development

Today most people live into old age. During their lives their bodies will keep changing and developing.

Over the next six pages we will look at five stages in our lives:

- infancy
- childhood
- **adolescence**
- adulthood
- old age.

Say again ?

Adolescence – this is the time when you change from a child into an adult

Infancy

Before a baby is born, it has been growing and developing. Most babies are born around 40 weeks after **conception**. How a baby grows and develops during pregnancy depends on its own unique genetic code and the health of its mother. This is why pregnant women have health check ups. After birth, a baby will need love, care and stimulation in order to grow and develop. In the first year of a baby's life, growth and development are fast.

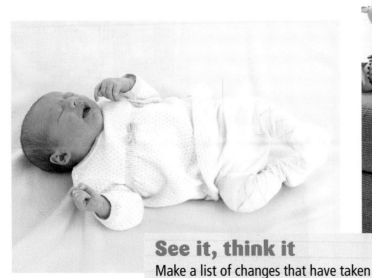

See it, think it
Make a list of changes that have taken place since this baby was born. Look back at pages 12–13.

Say again?

Conception – this is the moment the man's sperm enters into the woman's egg

Childhood

Childhood is a time when children learn the skills that they will need later for life. They do this by playing and also by being with adults. On pages 12–17 we looked at the first six years of childhood. After the age of 6 years, children's growth and development is slower. They now improve the skills that they have. An 8 year old can now run fast. A 10 year old will find it easier to read than a 6 year old.

Over to you...

Match up the skills to the different ages. Look at pages 12–15 to help you!

Can sit up	6 years
Can walk	18 months
Starts talking	2 years
Can play with others	9 months
Can read	3 years

See it, think it

What skills is this child learning by playing a game of snakes and ladders?

Guess what!

Identical twins share the same genetic code, but often develop differently because of life experiences.

From adolescence into adulthood

At around the age of 11, children's bodies start to change shape. They start to grow into adults. This process is called puberty.

Puberty

Puberty begins when the body starts making chemicals known as hormones. These chemicals make the body change. Girls will become women who can have babies. Boys will become men who can become fathers.

During puberty the body's shape changes dramatically.

Puberty — High five

1. Puberty takes four years.
2. Girls go through puberty before boys.
3. The body makes hormones so that it can change.
4. Young people will grow during puberty.
5. The brain changes during puberty.

Learning to be an adult

During adolescence young people's bodies are changing. Their brains are also changing. This means that they have their own ideas. They may also want to be more independent. During these years, they will sometimes act like adults, but sometimes they will act like children. This can cause problems at home and at school. For young people this can be a difficult period. Most young people find it easier to be with friends rather than with their parents.

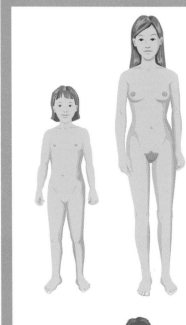

Girls begin to develop breasts and pubic hair. By the age of 14 years, most girls have begun their periods.

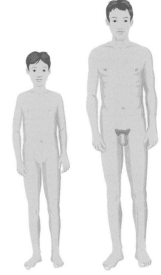

Boys develop facial and pubic hair. Their voices deepen and their sex organs develop. They grow quickly in height and weight and are, on average, taller than girls.

Guess what!

In the growth spurt that comes with adolescence, hands and feet grow first.

Adulthood

At the age of 18, the law says that people are adults. Adulthood is the longest part of our lives. In this time, our lives and bodies will keep changing. Here we look at the first part of adulthood.

A time of doing...

Most people will do many of these things by the time they are 50:

- get a job
- find somewhere to live
- meet a partner
- have a family.

How we age

From the age of about 25 our bodies begin to age. Some cells are not replaced and we produce fewer hormones. The good news is that our brains can keep developing if we keep doing interesting things.

Guess what!

Our brain does not stay the same throughout our lifetime. It changes according to our experiences.

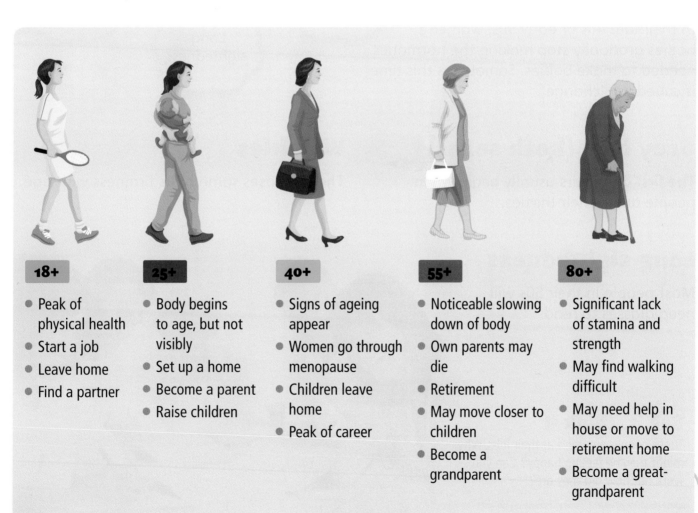

18+
- Peak of physical health
- Start a job
- Leave home
- Find a partner

25+
- Body begins to age, but not visibly
- Set up a home
- Become a parent
- Raise children

40+
- Signs of ageing appear
- Women go through menopause
- Children leave home
- Peak of career

55+
- Noticeable slowing down of body
- Own parents may die
- Retirement
- May move closer to children
- Become a grandparent

80+
- Significant lack of stamina and strength
- May find walking difficult
- May need help in house or move to retirement home
- Become a great-grandparent

Old age

As we get older, our bodies change. How quickly this happens is linked to the way that people live and their genetic makeup.

This means that some older people can be very 'young'.

Balding (men)

Some men start losing their hair in their 30s. Others will keep their hair, but it will go grey.

Menopause (women)

In their late 40s or early 50s, women's bodies gradually stop making the hormones needed to make babies. Sometimes this time is called the 'change'.

Balding

Menopause

Signs of ageing

Wrinkles

Grey hair

Long-sightedness

Grey hair (both sexes)

The first grey hairs usually begin when people are in their thirties.

Wrinkles

The skin loses some of its firmness with age.

Long-sightedness

Most people in their 50s will need glasses to read.

See it, think it

These people are good at their jobs. Why might they be feeling happy? Can you work out how old they are?

Middle age

The process of ageing is not sudden. Before old age comes, there is some time in the middle. This is known as middle age. For many people this is a good time in their lives. They may feel more confident than before. They may have a little more money to spend on themselves. Some may also have good jobs at this point in their lives. This means that many middle-aged people look and feel quite young.

Spot it
These older people are learning a new skill. Work out why it might be good for them.

Old age

It is hard to know when old age begins as many people today are living longer and retire quite late. Many people are also fitter and more active than before and so retire later.

Health problems

Older people are more likely to have health problems. This is because the body has slowed down and is not replacing and repairing cells. Some health problems are linked to the way that people live. Others are linked to their genetic makeup. Common health problems include:

- pains in joints
- Diabetes Type 2
- cancer
- hearing loss
- vision loss
- heart problems.

Active old age

Many people live an active old age. They can use the computer, go out with friends and keep busy. They may look after their grandchildren. Advances in health and technology mean that many people will not become 'old' until after they reach their 80s.

Keeping young   **High five**
1. Keep on exercising.
2. Get out and meet people.
3. Learn new skills.
4. Eat plenty of fruit and vegetables.
5. Cut down on smoking or drinking.

Areas of development

Growth and development is such a big topic that it is often split into different areas. For this unit, we are going to look at four areas.

Intellectual development

This is about the way that we can think. Thinking allows us to plan ahead, make choices and understand what is going on. The brain is responsible for our ability to think. From birth until the age of 20, the brain grows and develops. Even when we are adults, it changes and grows as we do, see, taste and try out new things. Older people can keep their brains working well if they do and see new things.

Physical development

This is about everything to do with our bodies. It is about the skills that we can use, but also about the way our body changes. Babies have to learn to control their bodies, while adolescents find that their bodies change shape. Older people find that they get tired more easily.

Emotional development

This is about how we can learn to control feelings such as anger and jealousy. It is also about feeling loved and loving others. Babies and young children are very emotional. They tend to cry easily, but also find it easy to smile and laugh. They need plenty of love and care from their parents. Adolescents can also be emotional. This is because the hormones needed to grow and develop also change the way they feel. In adulthood, people will have times when they feel happier than at others.

Social development

This is about getting on with others and understanding them. It is strongly linked to emotional development. It takes time to learn to share and play with others. Most children learn to do this from 3 years. Having friends and getting on with others is important at all ages of life. Some older people find that they become lonely. They may find it harder to get out and meet up with friends and people.

Having a healthy brain

High five

1. Try out new things.
2. Read.
3. Play games.
4. Meet people.
5. Keep physically active.

Spot it
Spot the three different emotions.

Factors that affect people's lives

If you ask an older person, they will tell you about many different things that have happened to them. Some of these will have affected their development.

Factors that affect physical growth and development

There are many factors that affect growth and development.

Diet

What you eat makes a difference at every stage of your life. Healthy food in the right quantities helps the body to fight infections. It also gives the body enough energy to do things such as walk and move around. How much food and what type of food you need changes as you get older. The wrong types of food or too much can put people at risk of illness.

See it, think it
The 80 year olds in this photo are still fit and active. What factors might have helped them?

Exercise

Even unborn babies take exercise. Our bodies need to move and be active. Exercise keeps muscles and the skeleton strong. Not enough exercise can make it harder to stay healthy.

Illness

Being ill can stop the body from growing and developing properly. Being ill may make people tired or stop them from being active. Some illnesses are bad luck or are linked to our genetic makeup. But some illness can also be a result of people not taking care of themselves. They may eat a poor diet, smoke or drink too much alcohol.

Sleep

At every stage in life, the body needs enough sleep. Sleep helps the body to fight illness and allows the body to repair or grow new cells. Sleep also helps the brain to stay healthy. How much sleep you need depends on your age. Babies may sleep for 12 to 14 hours, but adults need 7 to 8 hours.

Accidents

A serious accident can affect physical development. Losing a hand, eye or leg can make life much harder. This is why adults working with children must keep them safe. It is also why there is a lot of safety equipment around.

Circumstances that affect emotional and social well-being

How well we get on with others makes a big difference to how happy we feel.

Family

For most people, getting on with their family is important. Babies and children need to feel loved by their parents. In adolescence, relationships can be difficult. Later in life, many people will have their own children. Feeling close to them will be important.

See it, think it
These people are good friends. Why is having friends good for you?

Events that can affect our emotional and social well-being

High five

1. Death or illness of a family member, friend or partner.
2. Falling out with someone.
3. Being separated from people you like.
4. Being treated badly by a family member, friend or partner.
5. Losing a job.

Friendships

Having friends is important at all ages. Children like having friends to play with. As you get older, friends can share your problems, give you help, but are also there to have fun with. Falling out or losing a friend is hard. So is not being able to make friends.

Partners

Many people will have a partner during their adult years. Some people will marry and have children. Having a partner can make people very happy, but not getting on can cause problems. Separation or divorce can make people very angry, sad or lonely. Not having a partner when you want one can also be difficult.

Work

Most people find that working gives them money, but also makes them happy. Many people will make friends at work. Losing your job or not finding a job can make people lose confidence.

Effects of ageing in later life

Today many people live until they reach 80 years old or more. Doctors can also help people stay healthier for longer. This means that it is not until the last few years of life that the effects of ageing start to be a problem.

How fast people age is down to genetic makeup and also lifestyle. People whose grandparents lived into their 90s have a better chance of living longer. But it also depends on having a healthy lifestyle. Smoking, alcohol and a poor diet can cause early signs of ageing.

Emotional effects of ageing

Many old people do not like being old. They say that they feel young inside. They do not like needing help or being slower. They may not like the way that they look. This means that some older people can lose confidence.

Social effects of ageing

Many older people do not feel welcome in our society. Younger people can be impatient with them or rude. They can also feel lonely. Seeing family and friends can be difficult. They may not be able to walk or use public transport.

See it, think it
Oscar used to be a successful businessman. Now he needs help to move around. How might he feel?

Physical effects of ageing

Slowing down

Most people start to feel that their bodies are slowing down after the age of 60. This is true because the body does not repair or make new cells at the same rate. This means that they become tired more easily than before. Keeping active for as long as possible can slow down this process.

Speed of reaction

Many older people have to stop driving because they cannot react quickly enough. They may also not see well.

Respecting older people   **High five**

1. Give up your seat on the bus.
2. Be patient if they are slow.
3. Offer to lend a hand.
4. Smile and talk.
5. Take an interest in them.

Wear and tear

Some parts of the body wear out with age. Older people may find that their joints hurt or stiffen. This may make it hard to walk or do fiddly things with their hands.

Eyesight

With age, people's eyes change. Some people will need glasses but others may lose some or all of their sight.

Hearing

The cells in our ears are quite sensitive. Older people are likely to lose some of their hearing over time as the cells are not replaced. Young people can also lose their hearing early if they listen to loud music.

Dementia

Some older people develop an illness that affects the way their brain works. It makes them confused and forgetful. Doctors are trying to work out a cure for this.

Activity centre 3

1. Match up AC 1.1

Match the photographs to the main stages of human development.

Infancy
Childhood
Adolescence
Adulthood
Old age

2. Do it! AC 1.1, 1.2

Make a poster that shows the five different stages of human development. For each stage, write down one or two things about it.

3. True or false? AC 2.1

Which of these will make a difference to physical growth and development?

	True	False
Eating too much	☐	☐
Doing no exercise	☐	☐
Sleeping with a pillow	☐	☐
Smoking cigarettes	☐	☐

4. Remember me?   AC I.2

What are the four areas of development?

Look back on page 34 for more information.

7. Odd one out!   AC 2.3

All but one of these can be signs of ageing in older people. Find the odd one out!

Greying hair

Getting tired more easily

Watching television

Needing glasses

5. Agony page   AC 2.2

Why might a visit from Laura be good for her sister Ann?

I am worried about my sister, Ann. She has just split up from her boyfriend. She has moved town and has not made any friends. Should I go and see her? We do get on well.

Laura

8. Spot it!   AC 2.3

Look at these photographs. For each photograph, identify an area of development.

6. Do it!   AC 2.2

Make a poster showing three different life events that can affect a person's happiness.

3

Healthy living

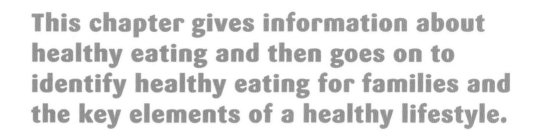

This chapter gives information about healthy eating and then goes on to identify healthy eating for families and the key elements of a healthy lifestyle.

The units covered in this chapter are:

CFC7 Eating healthily
CFC20 Healthy eating for families
HLI Healthy living

In this chapter you will learn about:

- the main food groups
- why it is important to eat food from the main food groups
- what forms a balanced diet
- what effects a balanced diet has on health
- the importance of family mealtimes
- ways to encourage children to eat healthily and what a healthy meal for a child is
- food restrictions due to religion and special dietary requirements
- how to prepare and store food safely
- the key elements of a healthy lifestyle and why it is important
- activities which contribute to a healthy lifestyle.

Main food groups

Food keeps us alive. Food can be split into different groups.

The picture below shows the five main food groups. These are:

- fruit and vegetables
- starchy foods
- meat, fish, eggs and beans
- milk and dairy foods
- foods and drinks high in fat and sugar.

See it, think it
Look at the food plate. Which foods can you eat a lot of? Which foods must you only have a little of?

Spot it
Which fruit and vegetables do you like? Do you eat five portions a day?

Fruit and vegetables

We need to eat at least five portions of these. Fruit and vegetables have important vitamins in them. When eaten with other foods, such as meat, they can give you iron.

Starchy foods

These should be in every meal. Starchy foods give you energy and some vitamins.

Starchy foods could include:

- bread
- pasta
- cornflakes
- rice.

Meat, fish, eggs and beans

We need some food from this group. These foods give you energy and protein. Protein helps your body to grow new cells.

These could include:

- boiled egg
- cod
- mince
- lentils
- baked beans.

Milk and dairy foods

Milk and dairy foods give you energy and protein. They also have vitamins in them.

We should eat some food from this group every day.

These could include:

- milk
- yoghurt
- cheese
- fromage frais.

Food and drinks high in fat and/or sugar

We need only a little food from this group. These foods give you energy, but many will not have vitamins or minerals in them. This is why it is better to eat mainly from the other groups.

These foods include:

- butter
- margarine
- fried foods
- cakes, chocolate and crisps.

Guess what!

The way foods are cooked can make them high in fat. Watch out for fried fish or fried bacon.

Foods that are high in sugar and fat

- Chocolate bars
- Chips
- Crisps
- Cola
- Cakes

Why we should eat food from each group

Food keeps us healthy. It can stop us from getting ill. It also gives us energy. But you cannot eat just anything. You need a **balanced diet**. This means eating the right amount from each of the food groups. This way you will get the vitamins, minerals and protein that you need as well as energy.

Say again?

Balanced diet – this is when you eat the right amount of food from each of the four main food groups

Making up a balanced diet

We have looked at the different food groups. Now let's look at how we put together the foods to make meals over a day.

Breakfast

This is the most important meal of the day. It is a good idea to eat some starchy foods and also have a drink. These breakfasts are good, but you should not put a lot of butter or margarine on the toast.

See it, think it
What do you have for breakfast? What food groups are you eating?

Breakfast I	Breakfast 2	Breakfast 3	Breakfast 4
Orange juice	Orange juice	Toast and butter	Cheese
Cornflakes and milk	Boiled egg	Banana	Bread and butter
	Toast and margarine	Glass of milk	Yoghurt

Main meal

Many people have a main meal at midday. A main meal should give you food from all of the groups. Remember that there should be plenty of fruit and vegetables to fill you up.

Main meal I	Main meal 2	Main meal 3
Vegetable curry with rice and lentils	Shepherd's pie with carrots and peas	Fish and chips
Fruit salad and ice cream	Fruit yoghurt	Chocolate bar
Water	Water	Cola

Tea time

Some people will eat a cold meal or a smaller meal later in the day.
Let's look at which ones are the best.

Tea menu I	Tea menu 2	Tea menu 3
Jacket potato	Ham sandwich with salad	Burger and chips
Baked beans	Apple	Cola
A little grated cheese	Carrot sticks	Cake
Pineapple slices	Yoghurt	

Activity centre 4

1. Match up AC 1.1

Match the photographs to the main food groups.

Starchy foods
Foods high in sugar and fat
Milk and dairy foods

3. True or false? AC 1.1

	True	False
You should not eat any fruit or vegetables.	☐	☐
Pizza and chips have a lot of fat in them.	☐	☐
Rice is a starchy food.	☐	☐
Yoghurt is a dairy food.	☐	☐

4. Odd one out! AC 1.1

These are reasons why you should eat food from each of the food groups. Which is the odd one out?

You will stay healthy
You will have more friends
You will feel better

2. Do it! AC 2.1

Make a poster that shows meals which are healthy.

Food groups

We all need food to live. It gives us energy and keeps us healthy. On pages 44–45 we looked at how food is divided into five food groups.

A balanced diet

A balanced diet means having the right amount of food from each of these groups. How much of each food group you need changes as you get older. Children need more food from groups 3 and 4 than adults. This is because they are growing fast. Their stomachs are small and so they will also need snacks from food groups 1, 2 and 5.

5 Foods high in fat and/or sugar

1 Starchy foods

Balanced diet

4 Fruit and vegetables

2 Meat, fish, eggs and beans

3 Milk and dairy

Over to you...

Work out what food groups the following meals cover.
- lamb and vegetable curry with rice
- cheese on toast
- beef and salad sandwich

See it, think it

Look at these two meals. Which one is for a toddler and which one is for an adult? What is the difference?

Spot it

Which of these foods are high in fat or sugar (or both)?

Why a balanced diet is good for you

Our bodies need many different vitamins and minerals as well as energy. We can get this from food. Foods such as fruit and vegetables give us vitamin C. This is needed to keep skin healthy. Foods such as milk and yoghurt give us energy and also calcium. This is needed for our bones. Eggs and meat can give us iron. This is needed in our blood. If we do not eat a balanced diet, we can get ill. Too much food, especially if it is high in fat and sugar, can make people put on weight. This can cause heart disease.

Over to you...

Think about what you have eaten in the last two days. Have you had five portions of fruit and vegetables each day? Have you had too many foods that are high in fat or sugar?

Food and the family

Food is important in families. Families need to eat together. Children need to learn about healthy food. They also have to be given food that is right for their age.

Family meal times

Family meals are important. They help the family to come together. This is important if everyone is busy doing different things in the daytime. At a meal everyone can talk and listen. They can talk about how they feel or what they have done. Families who have meals together are often happier. Children can also learn how to sit at the table and behave.

See it, think it
This family has not seen each other all day. Why is it important that they have a meal together?

Encouraging children to eat healthily

Our taste for different foods starts when we are children. Here are five ways that we can encourage children to eat healthily.

I. Give children healthy foods – for snacks, drinks and meals. Do not give children sweets, treats and crisps very often.

2. Show children that you eat healthy food. Children like to copy adults.

3. Cook with children. Children will often try the food that they have cooked. This is a good idea with vegetables.

4. Make sure that food looks good. You can make food faces.

5. Make sure that puddings are low in sugar and are healthy.

Healthy snacks — High five

1. Carrot sticks
2. Plain popcorn
3. Yoghurt
4. Banana
5. Fruit salad

Healthy meals for children

Adults should give children healthy food. Meals for children must have food from each of the food groups. A healthy meal for a child is shown below.

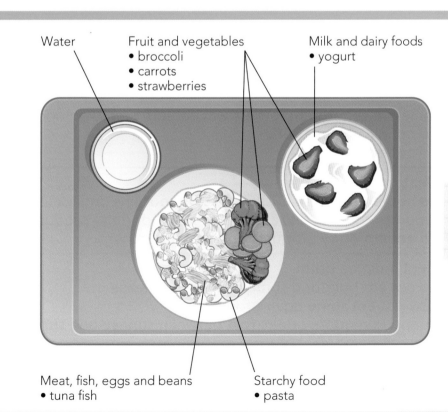

Water

Fruit and vegetables
• broccoli
• carrots
• strawberries

Milk and dairy foods
• yogurt

Meat, fish, eggs and beans
• tuna fish

Starchy food
• pasta

See it, think it
This is a healthy lunch for a child. Work out why.

Special diets

There are some foods that not everyone eats.
When planning meals, it is a good idea to find out
what people can and cannot eat.

Religious reasons

Some families are religious. Some religions
have rules about food. The table below
shows foods that some families will not eat.
Some religions also have rules about the
way food is made. Jewish and Muslim
families will only eat meat if the animal has
been killed in a certain way. Before giving
food to people, it is a good idea to check if
they have any special food needs.

Say again?

Kosher and **halal** – these are special ways of killing
animals
Fast – many religions have special times when food
is not to be eaten

Religious groups	Comments
Hindus	• Mainly vegetarian • Do not eat beef • May not eat some cheeses • Do not usually eat pork
Sikhs	• Some are vegetarian; others will eat lamb, chicken and fish • Do not usually eat pork • Do not eat beef
Jews	• Meat must be **kosher** • Do not eat pork, shellfish or fish without fins and scales • Separate cooking dishes must be used for dairy products • Do not eat dairy products and meat together
Muslims	• Meat must be **halal** • Do not eat pork and some do not eat cheese • May not eat some dairy products • During Ramadan, adults **fast** between sunrise and sunset
Rastafarians	• Mainly vegetarian, although some eat fish • Do not eat pork • May not eat some cheeses

Special dietary requirements

There are groups of people who may have other food needs.

Vegetarian

> I do not eat meat or fish. I will eat eggs and dairy products.

Diabetic

> I have a disease that means that I must be careful what I eat. I cannot have many sugary foods.

Vegan

> I do not eat any food that has come from an animal. I only eat food that comes from plants.

Food allergies

Some people cannot eat or touch some foods because they are allergic to them. Their skin might become red or they may find it hard to breathe. Food allergies can be very serious. This is why you must check before giving people food. Common allergies are:

- nuts
- cow's milk
- wheat (used in bread, pizza, pasta)
- egg.

Say again?

Vegetarian – eats food that is not made from killing animals
Vegan – eats food that is only made from plants

Find out!

Find out more about one of these groups of people.

Food safety

Food can make you ill if there are germs on it. This is called food poisoning. On this page we will look at how to keep food safe.

Handwashing

When making or serving food, you must first wash your hands. Do this with hot water and soap. This stops germs on your hands from going onto the food or onto the plates. It also stops germs from raw meat and fish from getting onto foods that are ready to serve.

Handwashing is needed   High five

1. Before you touch food
2. Before you touch plates, glasses, knives and forks
3. After you have been to the toilet
4. After touching raw meat or fish
5. After you have sneezed or coughed

Before handling foods you should always make sure you follow the points shown in the diagram.

Guess what!

Food poisoning can make you sick and give you diarrhoea.

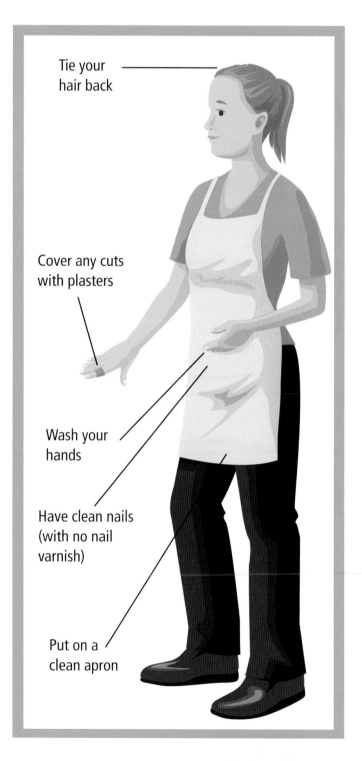

Tie your hair back

Cover any cuts with plasters

Wash your hands

Have clean nails (with no nail varnish)

Put on a clean apron

Hazards of poor storage and preparation

Where and how you keep food can cause a **hazard**. Food has to be stored properly for it to be safe.

Say again?

Hazard – this is about the way that something might be dangerous

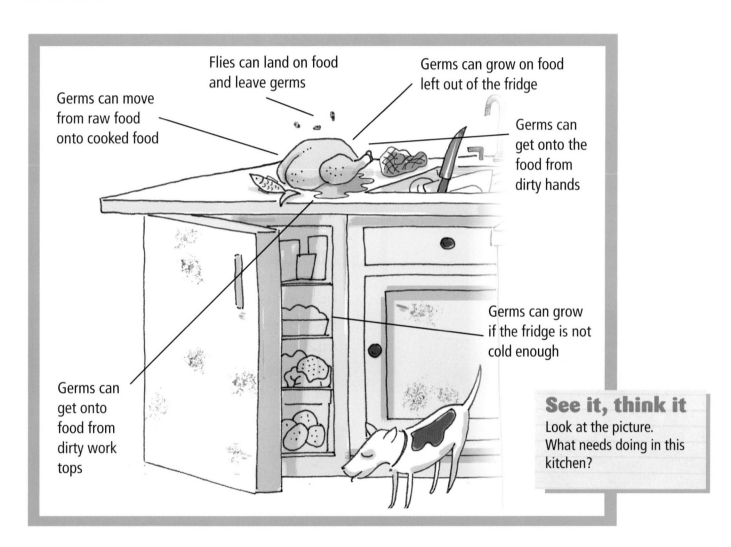

Flies can land on food and leave germs

Germs can grow on food left out of the fridge

Germs can move from raw food onto cooked food

Germs can get onto the food from dirty hands

Germs can get onto food from dirty work tops

Germs can grow if the fridge is not cold enough

See it, think it
Look at the picture. What needs doing in this kitchen?

Cross-contamination

When germs move from one place to another, it is called cross-contamination. There are several ways to stop this from happening.

1. Use separate chopping boards and knives for raw and cooked foods.

2. Do not store raw and cooked foods near each other (even in the fridge).

3. Wrap up cooked foods.

4. Cook raw foods well.

5. Keep the kitchen clean.

Activity centre 5

1. Do it!   AC 1.1, 1.2, 1.3

Look at this Eat well plate. It shows how much of the food groups an adult should eat.

Now:

- Write a list of meals and snacks that you have eaten recently.
- Work out which food groups are covered.
- Work out if you have had a balanced diet.
- Why is it important to have a balanced diet?

2. Do it!   AC 2.1, 2.3

Make a poster that shows families why meal times are important. On the poster show a meal that is healthy for children.

3. Odd one out!   AC 2.2

All but one are ways of helping children to eat healthily. Which is the odd one out?

Give them more pudding if they eat up their vegetables.

Sit and eat healthy food with children.

Let children help cook a healthy meal.

4. Spot it! AC 4.2, 4.3

Spot four hazards in the way that food is being stored and prepared in this kitchen.

5. Do it! AC 4.1, 4.2, 4.3

Make a poster that shows how to stop germs from getting onto food.

6. True or false? AC 3.1, 3.2

	True	False
Muslims eat Halal meat.	☐	☐
Sikhs and Hindus can eat beef.	☐	☐
Vegetarians do not eat meat.	☐	☐
Jews do not eat shellfish.	☐	☐
Vegans eat cheese and eggs.	☐	☐

7. Agony page AC 3.3

Explain which foods contain wheat. Give Dan an idea for a meal that his friend can eat.

My friend is coming for a meal. He cannot eat wheat. I am not sure what foods I can cook for him. Can you give me some ideas please?

Dan

Key elements of a healthy lifestyle

There are some things that you can do to keep yourself healthy and fit.

Diet ✔

What you eat and drink can help you to be healthy. We looked at the foods that are good for you on pages 44–45. Eating too much – even if it is healthy food – is not good for you. What you drink is also important. The body needs water.

Alcohol ✘

Too much alcohol can stop the liver from working. It can also make people put on weight. People who get drunk are more likely to have accidents or get into fights.

Keep healthy and fit
- Exercise ✔
- Smoking ✘
- Personal hygiene ✔
- Alcohol ✘
- Drug use ✘
- Relationships ✔
- Diet ✔

High five

Having a healthy lifestyle

1. Walk, jog or cycle.
2. Eat a healthy diet.
3. Do not smoke.
4. Do not use drugs.
5. Have a wash every day.

Smoking ✘

Smoking stops oxygen from getting into our bodies. This makes it hard for the lungs to work well. People who smoke find it hard to take exercise. Smoking also stops cells in the body from getting oxygen. It makes skin age faster. It can also cause heart disease and cancer.

Exercise ✔

Walking quickly or playing sport is good for the body. It keeps the bones in the body strong. It keeps the heart fit. It makes the lungs stronger. It also makes us feel better.

Guess what!

Adults need 30 minutes of moderate activity, five times a week. Walking quickly is enough.

Spot it

Look at the picture. Can you spot four reasons why this person is not having a healthy afternoon?

Personal hygiene ✔

Keeping clean is important. Skin can get infected if it is dirty. You have to wash your body and your clothes. People smell if they do not wash or if they wear dirty clothes.

Relationships ✔

We have to take care of our bodies if we have sex. It is possible to get infections very easily. Condoms can protect us from infections and also from getting pregnant. Sleeping around often makes people unhappy.

Drug use ✗

Drugs are chemicals. If they are not needed, they can change how the brain and body work. Even drugs such as cannabis (weed) can create mental problems.

The importance of a healthy lifestyle

A healthy lifestyle can make a difference to people's lives. They are less likely to get ill. They may also feel happier about themselves. They may live for longer. Let's look at some of the things that people say.

I don't smoke. I want nice skin and white teeth.

I don't use drugs. I can have a good time by just being with my mates.

I take exercise now. I've made lots of friends at the gym.

I take a shower every day. Then I know that I smell good.

Activities for a healthy lifestyle

There are many small things that you can do which will help you to become healthier.

Let's look at a few things you can do.

Diet

What you eat can make a difference to how you feel and to your weight.

Changing your diet — High five

1. Remember to eat a healthy breakfast.
2. Try to eat five portions of fruit or vegetables a day.
3. Avoid eating biscuits, crisps and chocolate.
4. Drink plenty of water.
5. Prepare healthy snacks, e.g. dried fruit, carrot sticks.

Fitness

Adults need to do 30 minutes of moderate activity, five days a week. You can do this in bursts of ten minutes if you like. Here are five things to think about.

1. Get off a bus one stop early and walk.
2. Walk or cycle to the shops or college.
3. Offer to take a friend's dog for a walk!
4. Try out a new sport.
5. Go swimming.

Smoking

Stopping smoking is the best thing that you can do for your body. There is no 'safe' number of cigarettes.

- Go to your doctor for help to stop smoking.
- Cut down on how many cigarettes you smoke.

Alcohol

Alcohol is not good for us. To stay safe, women should drink no more than three units a day. Men should drink no more than four units. You cannot save up units and drink them all in one night. This is called binge drinking and is very bad for the liver.

- Swap alcohol for a soft drink.
- Go somewhere where alcohol is not served.
- Do something different on the nights when you often drink.

1 unit of alcohol	• Pub measure of vodka, whisky or gin
1 and a half units of alcohol	• Small glass of wine • Bottle of alcopop
2 units of alcohol	• 1 pint of beer • 1 pint of cider • 1 pint of lager • Glass of wine (175ml)
3 units of alcohol	• 1 pint of strong beer • 1 pint of strong cider • 1 pint of strong lager

Drug use

Taking drugs is not good for you. It is also illegal. Having a criminal record could mean that you cannot work with children. If you take drugs you should seek help.

- See your doctor and get help.
- Visit the Talk to Frank website and get help.
- Keep away from people who use drugs.

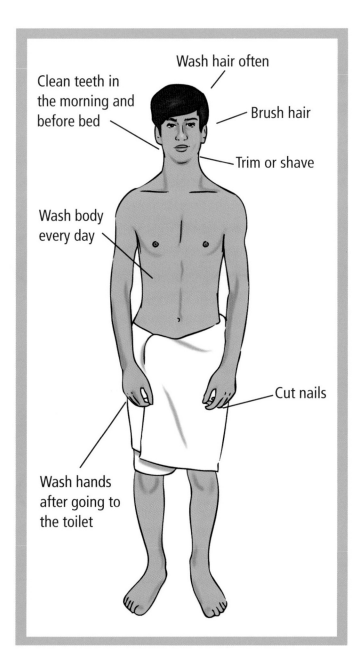

Wash hair often

Clean teeth in the morning and before bed

Brush hair

Trim or shave

Wash body every day

Cut nails

Wash hands after going to the toilet

Relationships

If you have sex, make sure you keep yourself safe.

- Make a visit to your sexual health clinic.
- Use condoms.
- Don't sleep around.

Personal hygiene

It is important to keep our bodies clean as well as our clothes.

Choosing activities

You need to think of three activities that will make you healthier. Choose ones that you know you can do easily.

Guess what!

Good personal hygiene
Cleaning your teeth twice a day, drinking plenty of water and not smoking will help keep your breath fresh.

Reviewing activities

When you make changes to your life, it is worth thinking about them. This is called reviewing.

Reviewing activities can be done in stages. This is what we are going to do here.

Reviewing activities → What went well → How the activities have improved lifestyle → Suggestions for the future

Reviewing activities → Areas for improvement

Carry out a review

To start off, think about how the activities you chose have gone over the past few days. Let's look at what three people say.

Jo: My boyfriend did not like using a condom. But he did it.

Sam: It was easy to walk to college.

Dan: I found it hard to stop smoking when I was with my friends.

Over to you...

Start thinking about how the three activities you chose on page 61 turned out.

Thinking about what went well

It is easy to think about what did not work out. But we need next to think about what went well. Let's go back to Dan, Sam and Jo.

Jo: I thought that getting condoms would be embarrassing. I found a local walk-in clinic. It was really easy. The condoms were free.

Sam: My friend started to walk with me. It did not take that long. One day, it was quicker than waiting for the bus.

Dan: It was easier to go to the 'Stop Smoking' clinic than I thought. The nurse was really nice. I did go two days without smoking.

Over to you...

Think about what went well for you. Do this for each activity.

Areas for improvement

When you review, you should also think about areas that you could improve. Let's go back to Dan, Sam and Jo.

Your lifestyle

Next, you need to think about how the activities have improved your lifestyle. Sometimes, changes or activities take time. But let's see what Dan, Sam and Jo say.

Over to you...

Work out what you need to improve on. Think about how you can do this.

Further activities

To keep healthy, you need to keep adding healthy activities to your life. Look back at pages 58–6I and work out what other things you could do or changes you could make.

Activity centre 6

I. Odd one out! AC I.I

Which is not a healthy activity?

Eating vegetables
Cleaning teeth
Smoking a roll-up
Having a shower
Swimming

2. Agony page AC I.2

Read the letter. Tell Jon why a healthy lifestyle is important.

There is a girl that I really like. I have asked her out, but she doesn't like me. Her friends say it's because I smell and smoke. Do you think that it really matters?

Jon

3. Match up AC 2.I

Look at these activities. Match them up to the key elements of a healthy lifestyle.

Walking	Diet
Eating fruit and vegetables	Relationships
Wearing clean clothes	Fitness
Not sleeping around	Personal hygiene

4. Spot it! AC 3.I

Can you spot the things that James needs to do to be healthy?

5. See it, think it

AC 2.I

Look at the picture. Can you spot the healthy activities that these people are doing?

6. Do it!

AC 3.4

Find out more about stopping smoking. Visit the NHS Smokefree website or visit your doctor. (To obtain a secure link to the website, see the Websites section on page ii.)

7. Do it!

AC 3.I

Keep a diary of how much exercise you take for a week. Do you do 30 minutes on five days a week? Work out how you could do more.

8. True or false?

AC 3.4

	True	False
Cleaning your teeth stops your breath from smelling.	☐	☐
Smoking stops you from getting pregnant.	☐	☐
Washing your hands can stop you from getting ill.	☐	☐
Eating fruit and vegetables will make your skin healthier.	☐	☐
Taking exercise makes you put on weight.	☐	☐

4

Keeping children healthy and safe

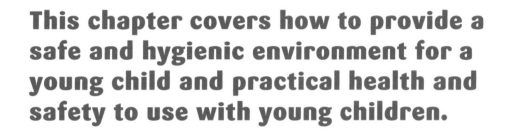

This chapter covers how to provide a safe and hygienic environment for a young child and practical health and safety to use with young children.

The units covered in this chapter are:

CFC3 Providing a safe and hygienic environment for a young child
CFC24 Practical health and safety when with young children

In this chapter you will learn about:

- daily personal hygiene for carers and young children and why it is important
- common signs of ill health in young children
- how to respond to ill health in young children
- possible hazards to a young child in the home
- how to prevent accidents to a young child in the home
- health and safety guidance, symbols and instructions on young children's equipment and toys
- health and safety instructions on home cleaning materials
- health and safety rules, guidelines or instructions when taking children out
- safety features, equipment or controls to ensure children are safe at home and outside
- fire safety equipment recommended for the house, possible fire hazards and how to maintain a child's safety if there is a fire.

Daily personal hygiene

We have to keep clean. We also have to keep children clean. Personal hygiene is about doing things every day to keep clean.

Let's look at ways to keep clean.

Good hygiene
High five
1. Good hygiene stops germs from getting into our bodies.
2. It stops germs from being spread to other people.
3. Brushing teeth stops teeth from rotting.
4. Children and adults smell if they are not clean.
5. Being clean makes children and adults look better.

Face
Faces need to be washed in the morning and at night. Children may need to wash their face more often because they may be messy when eating.

Hair
Hair needs to be washed often.

Teeth
Teeth need to be cleaned in the morning and at bedtime.

Hands
Hands need to be washed many times a day.

Whole body
Most children and adults will take a shower or bath each day.

Guess what!
Keeping skin clean can stop germs from getting into our bodies.

See it, think it
Look at the picture. How many of these do you do each day?

More about hands...

Hands need to be washed lots of times during the day.

The importance of personal hygiene

It is important for children to be clean. Germs cannot be seen, but are often on our bodies and hands. If we use our hands to eat food, the germs can move into our bodies. This will make us ill. Keeping the skin, hair and teeth clean can stop children from becoming ill.

Before cooking or serving food

Before eating any food

After eating, if hands are sticky

Wash your hands...

After playing outdoors

After going to the toilet

After messy activities

Spot it
Can you spot how germs on unwashed hands might spread to other people?

I HAVE NOT GOT TIME TO WASH MY HANDS.

TOILET

Ill health in children

From time to time, children can be poorly. It is important for you to know when a child is not well.

Let's have a look at some signs of illness.

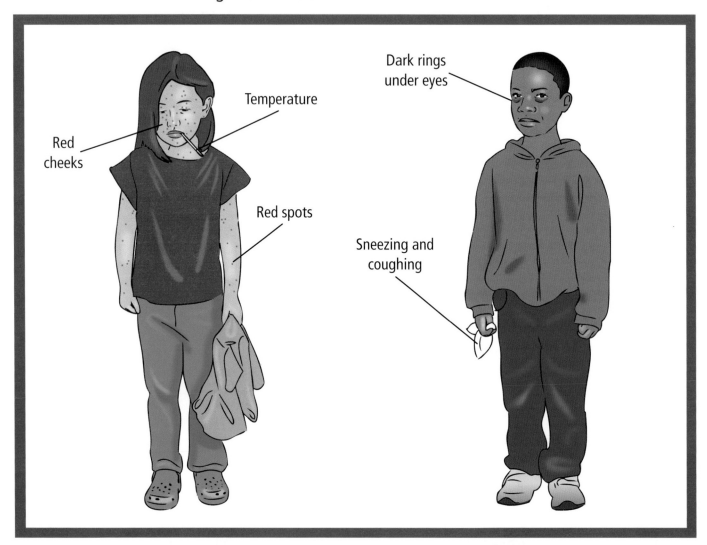

Red cheeks

Temperature

Red spots

Dark rings under eyes

Sneezing and coughing

Other signs to look for

Children who are poorly may not be hungry. They may cry or not want to play. Look out for children who only want to drink. They may have a sore throat. Some children may also be sick. This is a sign of being poorly.

Guess what!

A normal temperature is 36.9°C.

Responding to ill health

If we can see that children are poorly, we have to send for their parents or carers. We should also keep them away from other children. This stops germs from spreading. Being poorly is not nice for children. We need to be extra kind to them.

Spots

When children have spots they need to be seen by a doctor. Some spots and rashes can be serious.

High temperature

When a child has a temperature of more than 38°C, you need to get help. Make sure the child is not wearing a jumper or cardigan. Offer sips of water while you are waiting for help.

Sneezing and coughing

Try to get the child to use their hand or a tissue when coughing or sneezing to stop germs from spreading. They should wash their hands after blowing their nose, coughing or sneezing.

Being sick

Keep other children away. Wear disposable gloves to clean up. Wash the area well. Let the parents or carer know what has happened.

Not eating food

Never force a child to eat. They may be sick later. Tell the parents or carer about it.

When to call an ambulance — High five

1. If a child is finding it hard to breathe.
2. If a child has a temperature of 38°C.
3. If a child's skin has a bruise-like rash.
4. If a child is floppy or very drowsy.
5. If a child wants to get out of the light.

Accidents and hazards

Most accidents happen in the home. Babies and young children are at risk because they do not understand danger.

Babies and young children often pick things up out of interest. They may also try to copy things that adults do.

Hazards in the home

Spot it
Can you see the hazards in each of these rooms?

Bathroom/toilet

- Children may swallow or touch cleaning products.
- They may drink medicine.
- They may drown in bath water.
- If water is hot, it may burn children's skin.

Kitchen

- Children may swallow or touch cleaning products.
- Children get burns from kettles, pans and ovens.
- Children may cut themselves on knives.

Bedrooms

- Children may fall off a bed.
- They may open a window and fall out.

Stairs

- Children may fall down the stairs.

Living area

- Children may get burns from an iron.
- Children may touch hot drinks and get scalded.
- Children may touch cigarettes and matches and get burnt.
- Babies might fall out of highchairs.
- Children might touch the fire and get burnt.

Say again?

Scalded – when hot liquids burn skin

Preventing accidents   High five

1. Always keep an eye on young children.
2. Use safety equipment.
3. Always stay with children when they are near water – even only a little bit.
4. Keep everything tidy.
5. Lock away tools, cleaning things and medicines.

How to prevent accidents

Most accidents in the home can be stopped. There are many ways of doing this. One of the most important ways is not to leave children playing in rooms alone. Let's look at some other ways.

Room	Safety advice
Bedroom	<ul><li>Do not let children bounce on beds.</li><li>Make sure that toys are right for the age of the children.</li></ul>
Bathroom	<ul><li>Do not leave children alone in the bathroom.</li><li>Lock away medicine and cleaning things.</li><li>Make sure that the water is not too hot.</li></ul>
Kitchen	<ul><li>Keep children away from the cooker, knives and the kettle.</li><li>Lock cleaning things away.</li><li>Do not let children play in the kitchen.</li><li>Install child locks on cupboard doors.</li></ul>
Stairs	<ul><li>Put up stair gates.</li><li>Do not let children play on the stairs.</li><li>Help toddlers to climb safely up and down stairs.</li></ul>
Living area	<ul><li>Do not leave cigarettes or matches in the same room as children.</li><li>Do not let children play with plugs and electrical equipment.</li><li>Use a harness in a highchair.</li><li>Do not leave hot drinks around.</li><li>Use fire guards.</li></ul>

1. Remember me? AC 1.1, 1.2

Can you remember the daily hygiene activities that young children need? Why are they important?

3. Match up AC 1.1, 1.2

Can you match up the parts of the body to the boxes?

Teeth

> It has to be brushed once a day. It also needs washing often.

Hair

> You should brush them twice a day. This stops them from rotting.

Body

> It is important to wash everyday. It can smell if it is not clean.

4. Do it! AC 2.1

Make a poster that shows the signs of ill health in children.

2. Odd one out! AC 1.1

Washing hands

Which of these is the odd one out?

Wash hands after going to the toilet

Wash hands before cooking a meal

Wash hands before talking to a friend

5. See it, think it

AC 3.1, 3.2

Look at these pictures. Identify the hazards.
Work out how an accident can be stopped.

6. Agony page

AC 2.2

Read the letter and answer the
questions.

My son is 4 years old. He is
very hot. His skin is blotchy.
It looks like bruises. He is
screaming. What should I do?

Rani

1. Is this an emergency?
2. What should the mother do?

Guidance for health and safety

To keep children safe we have to read instructions. We also have to read warnings. On these pages, we look at some ways of keeping children safe.

Toy safety

It is important that the toys we give children are safe. There are several things to look out for. First of all, it is important that toys are right for the age of the child. If a child is not ready for a toy, they may have an accident with it.

If you see this on a toy, it means that you cannot let a baby or toddler play with it.

This sign is called a Lion Mark. It is good to see on a toy. It means it has been made by a member of the British Toy and Hobby Association. Their members make safe and quality toys.

This means that the toy meets European safety standards. $C\epsilon$

Instructions

As well as checking for symbols, look out for instructions. They tell you more about the toy or how it should be used.

Finding out more

If you keep the box or wrapper, you might be able to find out more about a toy. You can contact the maker.

Cleaning materials

Cleaning materials can make children ill. Some can poison them. It is important to keep all cleaning materials out of reach of children. Adults also have to use them safely. This means reading the labels. Let's look at some.

This sign tells you that the product is dangerous.

This tells you that this product is poisonous. It means that you should put it out of reach so that no one could drink it.

If this product touches your skin, it will harm it. You should wear gloves to use this cleaning material.

See it, think it
Can you see why this child might not be safe?

Taking children out

Keeping children safe is important when you go out. Let's look at how to keep children safe in the street and in the park.

Going to the park

You need to plan and get ready before going to the park. Make sure that children are dressed for the weather. Think also about whether a buggy is needed if it is a long way.

At the park

- Watch out for dog mess.
- Make sure that playground equipment is safe before letting children use it.
- Keep an eye out for strangers.
- Watch out for litter.

Keeping children safe in the street   **High five**

1. Keep young children on reins.
2. Hold older children's hands.
3. Keep children with you and don't let them run ahead.
4. Always use zebra or pelican crossings.
5. Talk to children about keeping safe.

Keeping children safe

Adults have to keep children safe. There are many hazards at home and when we go out.

We looked at some hazards in the home on pages 72–73.

Over to you...

Can you list four hazards that you might find in a living area?

Safety features

There are some safety features that can help to keep children safe in the home. You should always use them if you can.

Window locks

These stop children from opening windows and falling out.

Cupboard locks

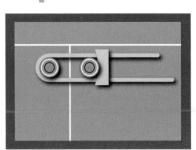

These stop children from opening cupboards.

Safety gates

These can stop children from falling downstairs. They can also stop children from going into the kitchen.

Fireguards

These can stop children from touching gas fires or hot radiators.

Corner guards

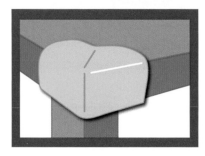

Some low tables have sharp corners. Corner guards can stop children from hurting their heads.

Plug covers

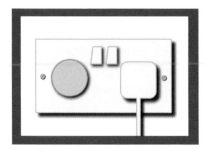

These can stop children from touching electric sockets.

Harnesses

These can stop children from falling out of high chairs.

Safety equipment and controls

We have to keep children safe when we go out. There is safety equipment and other controls that we can use in cars and in play areas for children.

Fluorescent strips and bands
These can be put on so that children and adults can be easily seen by drivers.

Safety on a walk

Harnesses and reins
These stop children from running into the road.

Zebra and Pelican crossings
These should be used when crossing busy roads.

Car child lock

Make sure that you put the child lock on. These are on the side of the car door. They stop children from falling out of the door when the car is moving.

Car seat

It is the law to use a child or baby car seat.

Make sure it is the right size for the child and follow the instructions. Car seats keep children safe if there is an accident.

All children under the age of 12 should be in a car seat.

Harnesses and reins

These can stop toddlers from getting lost.

Gates

Most playgrounds are fenced and have gates. Always close the gate so that young children cannot wander off.

Fire safety

Fire can kill children and adults. That is why we have to know how to keep children safe from fire.

Let's look at some of the ways we can keep children safe.

Fire safety equipment

It is possible to get fire safety equipment in homes.

Smoke detectors

These make a noise if there is a fire. They can save lives. Many local fire brigades fit them for free.

Fire blankets

These are used in kitchens. They are put over the top of saucepans if they are on fire.

Fire extinguishers

These contain chemicals to put out fires. There are different types of fire extinguishers. Some homes have one for the kitchen.

Fire hazards

A fire can start easily if we are not careful. Let's look at some of the hazards in a home.

Cigarettes

Cigarettes and matches cause many house fires. Ash from cigarettes can set fire to sofas, beds and carpets. You should try not to smoke in the home.

Matches and lighters

Some fires are caused by children playing with matches and lighters. They are often trying to copy adults. Never leave out cigarettes and matches where children can touch them. Do not use them in front of children.

Electrical faults

Electrical items can catch fire. Unplug the television and DVD when they are not being used. You should also turn off the washing machine and tumble dryer. Some fires are started because too many things are being run at once from the same plug.

Chip pans and deep fat fryers

Hot oil and fat can catch fire easily. You should never leave the room when using a chip pan or deep fat fryer. If they catch fire, you should put a fire blanket over the top. Never pour water onto hot fat.

Candles

Candles can cause fires. Do not use candles when children are around. If you light a candle, always stay in the room with it. Make sure that it cannot fall over. When you blow out the flame, check that it is really out.

Fairy lights

Fairy lights can catch fire. These should not be left on when you are not in the room.

Spot it
Can you spot the fire hazards in this room?

What to do in a fire

Once a fire starts, it can get out of control very quickly. If there is a fire, you need to act quickly to get everyone out safely. You should never try and put out a fire. This can waste time. Instead, get everyone out and then close the door of the room. You should never go back inside to get things.

Getting out quickly   High five

1. Call and shout so that everyone at home knows about the fire.
2. Take the children and leave the room. Close the door behind you.
3. Go out of the nearest door or window.
4. You have to get out fast and not waste time trying to get things out.
5. Once you are safely out, call 999. You could use a mobile, stop a stranger or go to a neighbour. Give the emergency operator the full address.

Activity centre 8

I. Remember me? AC I.I

Look at these symbols. What do they mean? (Look back at page 76.)

2. See it, think it AC I.I

Look at the instructions on the back of this packet. What must you do?

Kitchen Cleaner

Cleans grease and grime!

Instructions for use

Use product with caution.
Always wear gloves to apply.
Avoid contact with skin.

Keep out of reach of babies and children. Irritant

3. Do it! AC I.3

Make a poster that shows how to keep a child safe on a trip to the park.

4. Agony page AC 2.I, 2.2

Read Caz's letter. Make a list of things that Caz should get.

I am about to move into a new home. I want it to be safe for my toddler. What safety equipment should I get?

Caz

5. Spot it! AC 2.3

Can you spot the car seat for the baby? Why are car seats important?

7. True or false? AC 3.2, 3.3

	True	False
Cigarettes cause many house fires	☐	☐
You can put lots of adapters into a power socket	☐	☐
It is not a good idea to light a candle and leave the room	☐	☐
It is best to turn electrical items off at night	☐	☐
Smoke alarms can be turned off at night	☐	☐

6. Match up AC 3.I

Match up each piece of fire equipment to what it is used for.

Fire blanket

Used to make a noise if there is smoke in the home.

Smoke alarm

Used to put out fires. Often found in kitchens.

Fire extinguisher

Used in kitchens to put on top of burning fat or oil.

8. Do it! AC 3.3

Work out what you would do if there were a fire and you were with a child. What would you do first?

9. Do it! AC 3.3

Work out a plan to escape from your home if there was a fire in the kitchen. Work out which door you would use.

5

Care of children

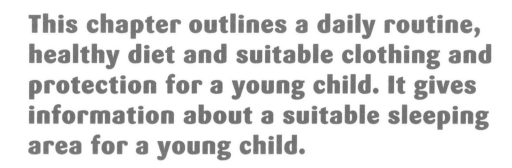

This chapter outlines a daily routine, healthy diet and suitable clothing and protection for a young child. It gives information about a suitable sleeping area for a young child.

The unit covered in this chapter is:

CFC4 Routines for a young child

In this chapter you will learn about:

- a daily routine for a child aged I to 2 years
- the benefits to a child of a routine
- a healthy diet for a young child aged 2
- clothing and protection for a child aged I to 2 outside in different weather
- the requirements of a sleeping area for a young child aged 2
- how different activities help to prepare a young child aged I to 2 years for bedtime.

Routines for young children

A routine is a pattern of things that we do each day. We will probably do them at the same time each day.

Let's look at things that must happen each day for young children.

Routines

Morning

Everyone needs to get up. Young children may need a nappy change. Everyone needs breakfast. Everyone needs to get washed. Toddlers will need their teeth cleaning.

Mid morning

Toddlers need to be busy. You can play with them or go outdoors with them. A toddler will also need a nappy change. They will also need a healthy snack.

Lunchtime

Everyone needs some lunch. Toddlers need food and a drink. After lunch most toddlers need a nap. It is a good idea to read a story before the nap.

Bedtime

Bath or shower time

Hand washing

Nappy changes

Lunch time

Daily tasks for young children

Time spent outdoors

Snacks

Time playing with adults

Tea time

Breakfast

Routines **High five**

1. Routines help children to sleep well.
2. Routines keep children healthy.
3. Routines help parents to know what to do.
4. Routines help children to be happy.
5. Routines help children to eat properly.

Spot it
Can you spot the things from the routine in this diagram?

Afternoon

Toddlers need a drink after a nap. They may like a small snack. They may need a nappy change. It can be good to go outside. Toddlers like going to the park. They like playing with adults.

Teatime

Toddlers get tired easily. They may want cuddles and to play. Then it is time for a meal. After tea, it is time to have a bath or shower.

Bedtime

After a bath or shower, it is time to clean toddlers' teeth. They will need a clean nappy as well. They fall asleep quickly if everyone is calm and quiet. You can look at books with them. Toddlers will need a good night hug and kiss.

The benefits of a routine

Routines are important for children. Young children need to eat, sleep and be kept clean. They also need to play with their parents or other adults. A routine makes sure that this all happens. It also makes children happy. They like to know what will happen. Routines are good for parents and adults. It helps them to plan their day.

A healthy diet

Children need to eat the right food to keep healthy. They also need the right clothing.

On these pages we look at what diet and clothing children need. Let's start by looking at food.

Food groups

We looked at the food groups on pages 44–45. Toddlers need food from all the groups, especially milk and dairy products. They do not need sweets, biscuits or cakes. They do not need crisps.

A diet for a 2 year old

Young children of 2 years cannot eat lots at a time. Their tummies are too small. Everything they eat should be good for them. They need three meals a day and two healthy snacks. Let's look at some healthy meals and snacks.

	Day 1	Day 2	Day 3
Breakfast	Egg and toast Cup of milk	Banana and yoghurt Cup of milk	Porridge Cup of milk
Lunch	Spaghetti bolognaise Peas and carrots Cup of water	Cauliflower cheese Strawberries Cup of water	Tuna, rice Sweetcorn Pineapple pieces Cup of diluted orange juice
Tea time	Cheese on toast with tomato Stewed apple Cup of milk	Fish finger and baked beans Chopped up grapes Cup of milk	Egg sandwich Banana Cup of milk
Snacks	Satsuma Small yoghurt	Raisins Slice of cheese and a cracker	Carrot sticks Bread sticks

Spot it
Can you spot how each menu has five portions of fruit and vegetables? What other food groups can you see?

See it, think it
Why has the food been chopped up?
Why is there not much food on the plate?

Adults have to choose the right clothes for children. Clothes need to be comfortable. They also need to be right for the weather.

Let's look at how we might dress a toddler.

Hot sunny day

When it is hot, we have to keep toddlers cool. We also have to stop the sun from getting on their skin. The sun can burn children's skin.

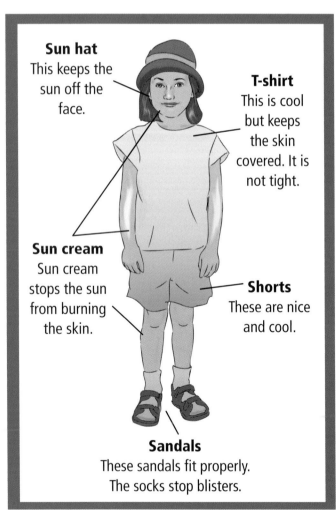

Sun hat
This keeps the sun off the face.

T-shirt
This is cool but keeps the skin covered. It is not tight.

Sun cream
Sun cream stops the sun from burning the skin.

Shorts
These are nice and cool.

Sandals
These sandals fit properly. The socks stop blisters.

Guess what!

Children's skin burns more quickly than adults' skin.

A rainy day

When it is raining, we need to keep toddlers dry. Toddlers like playing in puddles.

Raincoat
A waterproof coat keeps the child dry. A hood keeps the child's head dry.

Wellingtons
Boots keep the feet dry.

Socks
Socks keep the feet dry and comfortable.

Trousers
These keep the legs dry and warm.

Jumper
A jumper can be worn under a coat.

T shirt
A t-shirt can be worn under a jumper. It keeps the child warm.

Bitterly cold day

When it is cold, it is good to have many layers of clothing. It is also important to keep hands, head and feet warm.

Vest
Can be worn under a jumper. It is an extra layer.

T-Shirt

Can be worn under a jumper. It is an extra layer.

Jumper

This keeps the child warm.

Trousers

These keep the legs warm.

All in one

This can keep children warm when outdoors. They can run about in it.

Thick socks

Worn inside the boots, they keep the feet warm.

Boots

Boots are warm.

Hat

A hat keeps the head and ears warm.

Gloves

Gloves keep the hands warm.

Scarf

This keeps the neck warm. It stops the cold from getting in.

Windy day

When it is windy, we have to stop the wind from making children cold. We have to keep the head and hands warm.

T-shirt

This can be worn under a jumper. It is an extra layer.

Jumper

This keeps the child warm.

Trousers

These keep the legs warm.

Shoes and socks

These keep the feet warm.

Coat

This keeps the body warm.

Hat

This keeps the ears and head warm. It also stops hair from being blown around.

Scarf

This keeps the neck warm. It stops the cold from getting in.

Choosing clothing   High five

1. Make sure that it is right for the weather.
2. Make sure that it is comfortable.
3. Make sure that it is the right size.
4. Make sure that it is easily washed.
5. Make sure that shoes and boots fit properly.

Bedtime

Young children need sleep. They need a comfortable sleeping area. A sleeping area will help children to get to sleep.

Let's look at what children will need.

Safe

A child's **sleeping area** needs to be safe. Children often get out of their cots and beds. Never leave matches or medicine lying around.

Say again?

Sleeping area – this is a place where children can sleep (it may be their own bedroom or a shared space)

Clean and tidy

Children need clean bedding. They also need the area to be clean. Tidy spaces can stop accidents. Being tidy makes it easier to clean.

Right temperature

Rooms should be between 18 and 20°C. Too hot is not good for young children.

A cot or bed

Most children under 2 years old will be in a cot. Cots keep children safe. If a bed is used, it must be low.

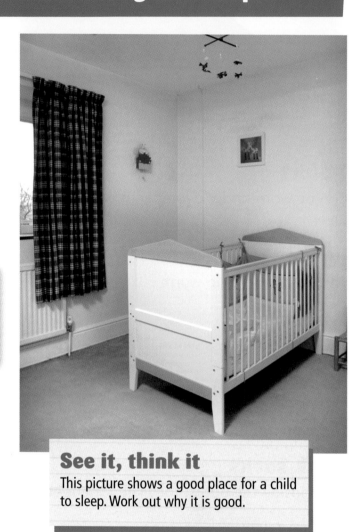

See it, think it
This picture shows a good place for a child to sleep. Work out why it is good.

Guess what!
It is easier to fall asleep in a dark room.

Getting children ready for bed

Bedtime routines can help children to fall asleep. Let's look at what we can do.

Bath time

A warm bath or shower helps children to relax. It makes them feel clean. Always check that water is not too hot. Never leave children alone near water.

Personal hygiene

Young children will need a clean nappy before bed. They will also need their teeth cleaning.

Clothing and bedding

Children will need comfortable night clothes. Most children wear pyjamas or sleepsuits. Clothes should be soft and easy for the child to move in. Young children will need to go into a cot. The sheets in the cot should be clean. In winter, children will also need blankets or a duvet.

Calming down activities

It is not a good idea to make children excited before bed. It makes it hard for them to sleep. Children need calm activities. Sharing a book with a child is a good idea, or talking to them about the day. You may also put on some soft music and sit quietly with the child.

Getting children ready for bed   High five

1. Have bedtime at the same time every night.
2. Get the sleeping area clean and tidy before bedtime.
3. Do the same things every night.
4. Be calm with children.
5. Make sure the room is safe.

Activity centre 9

1. Do it! AC 1.1

Make a poster that helps parents to know what a daily routine looks like for a toddler.

2. Agony page AC 1.2

Explain to Kyle why a routine might help.

My son is nearly 2 years old. We do not have a routine. He is often tired. We get cross with him. Do we need a routine?

Kyle

3. Remember me? AC 2.1

Can you think of the five food groups?

4. True or false? AC 2.1

Which of these are not true?

	True	False
Toddlers do not need snacks.	☐	☐
Toddlers have small tummies.	☐	☐
Crisps are good for toddlers.	☐	☐
Toddlers need small meals.	☐	☐
Toddlers need milk and dairy products.	☐	☐

5. Odd one out! AC 4.2

Getting ready for bed

All but one of these will help toddlers get ready for bed. Which one is it?

Bath time

Quiet story

Bouncing on bed

Cleaning teeth

6. Match up
AC 3.I

Match the photographs to the sentences.

I am dressed for the sun.
I am dressed for the cold.
I am dressed for rain.
I am dressed for a windy day.

7. Spot it!
AC 4.I

Look at this sleeping area for a toddler. Can you find five things that are not good?

8. Agony page
AC 4.I

Explain to Jaz why calming activities work well at bedtime.

At bedtime, my boyfriend bounces our toddler up and down. My toddler loves it, but then does not go to sleep. Does this matter? What other things could we do?

Jaz

6

Communicating with children

This chapter gives information about listening to and talking with a young child and how to respect and value children.

The units covered in this chapter are:

CFC2 Listening to and talking with a young child
CFC9 Respecting and valuing children

In this chapter you will learn about:

- ways an adult can be responsive and use active listening when listening to a young child
- activities for listening to and talking with a 2-year-old child, the role of the adult in these activities and the active part taken by the child in each of these activities
- ways to value children as individuals
- reasons why children need to be respected as individuals
- ways to communicate with children to ensure that they feel valued
- behaviour that shows respect and value of children
- organisations that promote the rights of children.

Let's look at ways in which we can listen to children.

Being responsive

Children of all ages need adults to be **responsive**. They need adults to show interest in them. This helps them to talk. There are many ways of being responsive to children.

Say again?

Responsive – this is about showing that you are interested

Guess what!

Young children often talk more when adults are close by.

Smile

Be interested

Being responsive

Make eye contact

Be on the same level as the child

Helping babies　　**High five**

1. Smile when a baby babbles.
2. Make eye contact as you talk to a baby.
3. Point out things to a baby.
4. Talk back to a baby even if you do not understand them.
5. Talk while you are doing things with the baby.

Active listening

Active listening is a set of skills. Adults who are good listeners use these skills. You can learn these skills. They help you to work well with children.

Active listening skills

- Make eye contact. You should look at the child but do not stare.
- Repeat back what the child has said; this will help the child hear it correctly.
- Smile and nod.
- Ask questions to show interest.
- Show that you are not in a rush – you could sit down with a child.
- Reply immediately if a child asks a question.
- Make comments that show that you have listened.

Say again?

Active listening – a set of skills to help people learn to listen

Over to you...

How do you know that someone is listening to you?

See it, think it

Look at this photograph. How can you tell that the adult is responsive to the child?

Activities for listening and talking with 2 year olds

Toddlers are still learning to talk. They need adults to help them. Adults need to listen to them and also help them to talk.

There are many ways that we can help toddlers to talk. Let's look at some.

Sharing books

Using puppets

Activities for listening and talking with 2 year olds

Nursery rhymes

Cooking

Role of the adult

Adults need to make sure that they are letting children talk. They also need to make sure that the activity is fun.

Children need to be active

Young children learn best when they can join in. Good activities let children join in. They may talk, hold something or ask questions.

Sharing picture books

Toddlers like looking at books. Choose a book with a simple story. Look for books with good pictures.

What the adult needs to do

- Help the toddler to choose the book.
- Help the toddler to look at the pictures.
- Talk to the toddler about the story.
- Let the toddler take their time looking at the book.

How the toddler can join in

- The toddler can point at pictures.
- The toddler can turn pages.
- The toddler can talk about the pictures.
- The toddler can choose the book.

Guess what!

You can use books with babies.

Using a puppet

Toddlers like puppets. Choose a clean puppet. Practise with it before showing it to a toddler.

What the adult needs to do

- Show the puppet slowly to the toddler.
- Make the puppet move slowly.
- Make the puppet do silly things.
- Tell the toddler what the puppet is saying.
- Let the toddler talk to the puppet.
- Talk back to the toddler.

How the toddler can join in

- The toddler can point at the puppet.
- The toddler can talk to the puppet.
- The toddler can ask questions about the puppet.
- The toddler can laugh at the puppet.

Cooking

Toddlers like helping to cook. Make sure that you choose safe and healthy foods. Get things ready first. Make sure that the area is safe and clean. Wash everyone's hands.

What the adult needs to do

- Let the toddler help.
- Talk to the toddler about what you are doing.

- Listen to what the toddler says.
- Point out things to the toddler.

How the toddler can join in

- The toddler can hold food.
- The toddler can mix.
- The toddler can talk about cooking.
- The toddler can ask questions.
- The toddler can listen.

Nursery rhymes

Nursery rhymes can help toddlers' speech. They like ones with actions. You will need to learn the rhymes first.

What the adult needs to do

- Say the rhyme clearly.
- Say the rhyme so that it is interesting.
- Repeat the rhyme.
- Allow the toddler to join in.

How the toddler can join in

- The toddler can join in the rhyme.
- The toddler can listen to the rhyme.

Favourite rhymes   **High five**

1. Two little dickie birds
2. Humpty Dumpty
3. Row, row, row the boat
4. Incey Wincey spider
5. Hickory Dickory Dock

Activity centre 10

1. Match up
AC 1.1

Responding to children

Match up the photographs to the skill.

Making eye contact
Being on the same level
Smiling
Showing interest

2. True or false?
AC 1.2

Active listening

Which of these are not examples of active listening?

	True	False
Looking at a child	☐	☐
Interrupting a child	☐	☐
Telling a child to speak clearly	☐	☐
Asking a question out of interest	☐	☐
Sitting with a child	☐	☐

3. Do it!
AC 1.2

Make a poster that shows adults how to be active listeners.

4. Odd one out!　AC 2.1

All but one of these activities will help children to talk. Which is the odd one out?

Sharing a story
Playing loud music
Finger rhymes
Talking with a puppet

5. Do it!　AC 2.1

Learn three new nursery rhymes.

6. True or false?　AC 2.2

	True	False
The role of the adult is to get children to sit still.	☐	☐
The role of the adult is to listen to children.	☐	☐
The role of the adult is to let children talk.	☐	☐
The role of the adult is to get children to repeat a word three times.	☐	☐

7. Do it!　AC 2.1, 2.2

Make a poster that gives adults ideas for listening and talking activities. Give ideas as to what the adult should do.

8. Agony page　AC 2.3

Read Jasmeena's letter. Explain how Aisha can take part in looking at books.

> My daughter, Aisha, is 2 years old. She cannot read. How can she join in when we are sharing books?
>
> Jasmeena

Children as individuals

Adults working with children need to value them. This means making every child feel special. It means making every child feel that they are cared about.

Let's think about how we can value children.

Greeting

Saying hello to a child helps them to feel special. It means that we have noticed them. It means that we are taking time to be with them.

Planning activities

If we plan activities for a child, it shows that we have thought about them. It might mean putting out a favourite toy. It might mean going out to the garden to look for spiders if that is what they are interested in.

Remembering special days

Some days are special for children. It might be their birthday. It might be a day when they are going to see their grandparents. It might be a special day for their family's religion. Showing that you have remembered a special day makes children feel valued.

Sense of belonging

It is nice if children feel that they belong. Having their own coat peg or drawer can make children feel special. Children may have their own plate or cup. This helps children feel valued.

Time

Children of all ages need time with adults. They need time to talk and to play. When children have time with adults that they like, this makes them feel special.

Over to you...

What kinds of things make you feel special?

Spot it

Can you spot how each peg is named? This helps children to feel as if they belong.

Why children need to be respected as individuals

While we need to care equally about every child, it is important to respect each one individually. This might mean that we work with them differently. One child might need more help than another. One child might like different toys from another. Let's look at why it is important to respect children.

Children's needs can be met

Children are more likely to be happy

Respecting children as individuals

Children are more likely to show positive behaviour

Children are more likely to care about others

Children are more likely to learn

Valuing children

One way of valuing children is the way that we talk and communicate with them. There are ways of doing this to make children feel valued.

Let's look at some of the ways in which we can show we value children.

Communicating with children

Listening	Children need adults to listen carefully to what they are saying. Adults who listen well think hard about what children are trying to say. They do not interrupt all the time.
Making eye contact	Looking at children as they talk is a way of valuing them. It shows that you are interested in what they are trying to say.
Voice tones	The way we speak can show children whether we like them or not. Bored tones do not make children feel valued.
Showing interest	Adults who value children show interest in what they are doing and saying. They notice what children are doing.
Playing with children	Playing with young children is a way of valuing them. It is important to let the child decide what and how they want to play.

Behaviours that show respect and value

The way that adults work with children can show them respect. A good way to work is to think about how you would like to be treated. Would you like to go to the toilet by yourself? Would you like a choice of what to do? Would you like to have a say in what is happening? These are the kinds of things that matter to children too. The spider diagram opposite shows how adults should behave.

Organisations that promote the rights of children

Children have many rights. They have the right to be treated well. There are many organisations that support children's rights. Let's look at some.

Unicef

This is an international charity that promotes children's rights.

NSPCC

This is a British organisation that tries to stop children from getting hurt by adults.

Allow children some privacy, e.g. going to the toilet

Let children do things for themselves, e.g. feeding themselves

Showing respect

Let children have a say, e.g. telling us about their ideas

Let children have some choices, e.g. choosing toys to play with

Citizens' Advice Bureau

This is an organisation that helps children and families by giving advice.

Children's commissioners

These are people who are meant to listen and stand up for the rights of children. There are commissioners in England, Scotland, Wales and Northern Ireland.

See it, think it
This child is choosing what to play with. Why is it important that adults let them do this?

Activity centre II

1. Match up AC 1.1

Match the photographs to the sentences.

Say hello to each child.

Take time to talk to each child.

Think about what each child likes playing with.

Remember children's special days.

2. Do it! AC 1.1

Make a poster that helps adults know how they could value children. Try and put some pictures on it.

C

3. Case study AC 1.1, 1.2

Read about Shona:

Shona has started nursery. She loves going every day. An adult always waits for her at the door. The adult says hello and talks to her. Her mum says that there are toys and activities put out that Shona likes. Shona also likes having her own coat peg. She feels very happy.

Now answer these questions:

1. How is this nursery valuing Shona?
2. How is this helping Shona?

4. Odd one out!   AC 2.1

All but one of these are ways to communicate with children and make them feel valued. Which is the odd one out?

Listening to what children say.
Interrupting children.
Smiling and showing interest.
Joining in their play.

5. Do it!   AC 2.2

Make a poster that shows adults how they can respect children. Make sure that your poster has some practical ideas!

6. True or false?   AC 2.2

Some behaviours do not show respect for individual children. Choose True or False for each of these.

	True	False
Shouting angrily shows respect.	☐	☐
Giving children choices shows respect.	☐	☐
Giving children privacy when on the toilet shows respect.	☐	☐
Making all the children do the same shows respect.	☐	☐

7. Do it!   AC 3.1

Find out more about UNICEF. They promote children's rights.

To obtain a secure link to the UNICEF website see the Websites section on page ii.

Play and learning

This chapter covers play and learning activities for babies and children and how adults can support them to play and learn safely and successfully.

The units covered in this chapter are:

CFC1 Confidence building for the young child through play
CFC5 Play and learning in the home
CFC13 Sharing learning experiences with children
CFC17 Supporting babies to play
Understanding play for early learning

In this chapter you will learn about:

- play activities that help build a child's confidence
- examples of activities that support a child to express their feelings and how interaction can help to build a child's self-esteem
- home-based play opportunities for babies and young children
- ways that children can learn and use their senses to find out about the world
- stories and rhymes for children aged 0 to 5 years
- objects of interest from the natural world and natural environments which may be used to extend children's experiences
- examples of how outdoor experiences can develop children's curiosity
- ways that babies' and children's physical, social, emotional, intellectual and language development is supported by play
- how individual needs of babies can be supported through play
- the adult's role in ensuring that babies can play safely and how adults encourage babies to play
- features of a setting that contribute to a positive learning environment and how these features help children to learn
- how a given set of materials, resources or activities might reinforce or challenge stereotyping and discrimination.

Play activities

Confidence is important for young children. When children are confident they will try out new things. They will also learn more easily.

There are many play activities that can help children. The best ones allow children to be in control. Let's look at a few.

Small world play
Train sets – farm animals – cars

Dressing up
Hats – shoes – coats

Activities to build confidence

Outdoor play
Climbing – riding bikes – running around

Junk modelling
Making things out of boxes, paper and glue

Spot it
Can you spot the children on the climbing frame? Why might this play activity help their confidence?

Supporting children

Sometimes children need help when they are playing. It is good to offer help. This makes the child feel that they are still in control. Sometimes children need us to be interested in what they are doing.

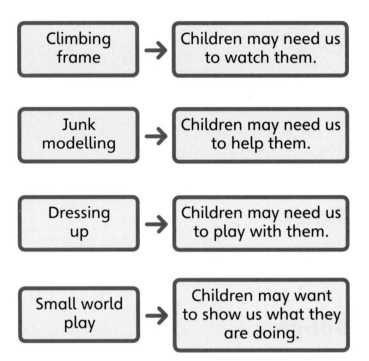

Climbing frame	→ Children may need us to watch them.
Junk modelling	→ Children may need us to help them.
Dressing up	→ Children may need us to play with them.
Small world play	→ Children may want to show us what they are doing.

Top tips

Helping children's confidence

- Toys and activities need to be right for children's age and stage.
- Praise children when they do things for themselves.
- Don't rush children when they are playing.
- Join in with children's play, but don't take over.

Find out!

There are many different types of small world play. See how many you can find out about.

Useful things for junk modelling

High five

1. Small boxes
2. Cardboard
3. Glue
4. Paint
5. Cardboard tubes

Expressing feelings

If children can express their feelings, this can help their confidence. Some activities let children show their feelings.

Activities that let children show their feelings can help children who are not talking. Let's look at some activities.

Puppets

Children like talking to puppets. Puppets can also make them smile and laugh.

Painting

Children like painting. Children can use paint to express their feelings.

Music

Children like making sounds. Children can make sounds that seem angry or happy.

Dough

Children like the feel of dough. If they are angry they can squeeze it. They can also pinch and hit it.

How interaction can help self-esteem

What we say to children is important. It can help their confidence. It is important to tell children that we are pleased with them. When we do this we are praising children. It is also important to be careful not to get angry with young children. This can make them feel worried. If adults are often angry, children can lose confidence.

Activity centre I2

I. Match up   AC I.I

Match the photographs to the activities.

Outdoor play
Dressing up
Painting
Junk modelling

2. Do it!   AC I.2

Make a poster that gives adults ideas for how to help children's confidence during one of the following types of play activity: outdoor play, dressing up, small world play or junk modelling.

3. Odd one out!   AC 2.I

All but one of these activities can be good for helping children to express their feelings. Which is the odd one out?

Playing with dough
Painting
Listening to an adult
Talking to a puppet

4. Do it!   AC 2.I

Make a poster to show adults some activities that are good to help children express their feelings.

5. Agony page   AC 2.2

Can you tell this mother why it is important to praise?

My mother says that I should praise my child more. I can't see why I should. What difference will it make? I'm just worried that he will get big-headed or become spoilt.

Jackie

Play opportunities

Babies and toddlers learn through play. They like playing with adults at home. This helps them to stay safe. Playing with adults also helps them learn to talk.

Let's look at some ways that we can play with babies and toddlers.

0 to 6 months

Baby gym

Babies can kick and touch the baby gym. They can enjoy looking at the shapes and colours.

Finger rhymes

Babies like playing with adults. Try saying 'Two little dickie birds' or 'Pat a cake'.

Gentle rocking

Babies like being rocked by an adult. Try rocking a baby gently. This is play for a baby.

6 months to 1 year

Pop-up toys

Babies like pushing buttons. Pop-up toys help babies to use their hands.

'Peepo' games

Babies like playing 'peepo' with adults. Try hiding your face with your hands. Then take them away and say 'peepo!'. Repeat this several times.

Knock-down play

Babies like knocking down beakers. Make the beakers into a tower. Let the baby knock them down.

1 to 2 years

Saucepan and spoons

Toddlers like making noises. They also like putting objects inside things. Try putting out a saucepan and some wooden and metal spoons.

Face cloths and water

Toddlers like playing with water. Put some water into a washing-up bowl. Put it on the floor with some face cloths. Do not leave the toddler alone with water.

Pegs and boxes

Toddlers like playing with clothes pegs. Put out a small box and some clothes pegs. See if the toddler enjoys putting them in and taking them out. Stay with the toddler while they are playing.

Ways that toddlers play **High five**

1. Opening and closing doors and boxes.
2. Dropping things.
3. Moving things from place to place.
4. Putting things in and out of sight.
5. Pouring and stirring things.

Supporting play in the home

There are many ways that we can support play in the home. Young children need a lot of adult time and attention. They also like to repeat play that they are enjoying.

Let's look at how we can support play.

Patience

Adults have to be patient. Young children often take time to do things. They often like to repeat games and play.

Offering help

Toddlers often need a little help. They like to do things by themselves, but may want just a little helping hand.

Being interested

Toddlers like being close to adults as they play. They like adults to take an interest in what they are doing.

Talking

Play can help children to learn. Talking to children as they play can make them learn more.

Providing choice

Toddlers can get bored after a little while. It is a good idea to be ready with another toy or activity. This means that adults have to be well organised.

Choosing toys that are right for them

Toddlers need us to choose toys that are right for them. They must be right for their age or stage of development. Toys that are too difficult will make them cross.

Making sure that toys are safe

High five

1. Read the label on packaging.
2. Choose toys that have safety marks.
3. Remove toys that are broken.
4. Check that the toy is right for the age/stage of child.
5. Stay with children as they play.

Adult responsibilities

Adults have responsibilities when children are playing. One of the most important is to keep children safe. We can do this in many ways.

Check that toys are safe

Supervise children

Adult responsibilities

Check what age the toys can be used

Do not leave children near water

Check that toys and objects cannot be swallowed

Spot it
Can you spot how this adult is supporting this toddler's play?

1. Match up

AC 1.1

Match the photographs to the age of children

Baby aged 3 months
Baby aged 10 months
Toddler aged 18 months

2. Do it!

AC 1.1

Make a poster that will give parents ideas about play in the home.

3. Agony page AC 1.1

Give this parent some ideas for how to play in the home.

My son is 1 year old. We do not have much money for toys.
Does this matter?
Can he still play?

Svetlana

4. Odd one out! AC 2.1

Supporting young children's play

All of these but one are ways to support children's play. Which is the odd one out?

Be patient
Ignore the child
Be interested
Talk to the child

5. Case study AC 2.1, 2.2

C

Jan looks after Daniel in her home. Daniel is 10 months old. She has found a shoe box and has put lots of spoons inside it. Daniel is having fun taking out the spoons one by one. Jan is sitting with him and talking to him. When he shows her a spoon she smiles. Jan is making sure that Daniel is safe.

1. What is Jan doing to support Daniel's play?

2. What responsibilities does Jan have?

6. Do it! AC 2.2

Make a list of ways in which adults can keep young children safe when they are playing.

How children learn

Adults working with children need to understand how children learn. This helps them to put out toys and plan activities.

Let's start by looking at some ways in which children learn.

Watching and copying others

Young children learn by watching and then copying.

A child might see another child digging in the sand. He might then start to copy the child's actions. Children will only watch and copy if they are interested.

Trial and error

Children learn by doing things for themselves.

A baby in the highchair may drop a spoon on the floor. The baby learns what happens when you drop things.

Repeating actions

Young children like to repeat play and actions that they enjoy. This helps them to practise skills.

A child might spend a while making sandcastles over and over again.

Discovery

Children like trying out new things. This is called discovery.

A child might see that an ice cube does not sink in water.

Spot it
This child is learning. Can you spot how she is also busy?

How children use their senses

Children use their senses to learn and find out about the world. Let's look at how they might use them.

Taste

Babies use their mouths to explore at first.

This baby is learning about texture by mouthing this spoon.

Touch

Babies and children need to touch things.

This child is enjoying the feel of dough. She is learning that it is soft and elastic.

Sight

Babies and young children like looking at things.

This child is looking at a snail. She is learning that snails do not have legs.

Sound

Babies and young children are interested in noises and sounds.

This child has now learned to make sounds with a shaker.

Smell

Babies and young children are interested in how things smell.

This boy has learned that some flowers smell.

Children need to investigate

Children are naturally curious. They like seeing what things can do. They like touching and smelling things. Babies and toddlers also put things in their mouths. It is important for children to explore and investigate. It helps them to learn. This is because they are using their senses. This helps them to remember things.

Using stories and rhymes

Children love stories and rhymes. They also help children's speech. Children who have heard many stories and rhymes find it easier to learn to read.

Let's look at some good stories and rhymes.

Stories for babies

Babies' first books are mainly pictures. Look out for books that have simple pictures of things that they might recognise such as baby clothes or a beaker. You might also look for books with simple animal pictures.

Rhymes for babies

Babies like simple finger rhymes and also action rhymes. You could try 'Two Little Dickie Birds' and 'Pat a cake, Pat a cake'.

Stories for toddlers

Toddlers like simple stories. They like repeating sentences so they can join in. They like stories about people and animals.

Rhymes for toddlers

Toddlers like rhymes that have actions. Try 'Humpty Dumpty' and 'Ring a ring a roses'.

Stories for young children

Children like stories that are about other children. They like to look at the pictures and talk about what is happening.

Rhymes for young children

Children like rhymes that are funny or sound funny. Try 'Five Fat Sausages' or 'Incey Wincey Spider'.

Sensory aids to support stories

We can help children to enjoy stories by using puppets. We can also use picture cards or real objects. As we are reading the story we can show children the puppet or they can hold the cards or objects.

Say again?

Sensory aid – something that helps children understand what is happening during a story or song

Helping children to take part

There are many ways that children can take part in stories and rhymes. Let's look at some.

Using a puppet

High five

1. Choose a puppet that links to a book.
2. Practise with it first.
3. Try to get it out without children seeing.
4. Try to move it slowly.
5. Let children talk to it.

Guess what!

Children don't mind if adults are not good at singing!

Stories

- Let children hold the book
- Let children choose books
- Put out sensory aids for children to hold
- Let children point to pictures in books
- Let children join in with sentences that they know

Rhymes

- Let children finish off rhymes
- Let children choose rhymes to sing or say
- Choose rhymes that have actions that children can join in
- Put out sensory aids for children to hold

Spot it
This girl is hearing the story of Three Billy Goats Gruff. Can you spot the sensory aids?

The natural world

For years children have learned by playing outdoors and with things that are found outdoors.

Let's look at some objects from the natural world that children can use in their play.

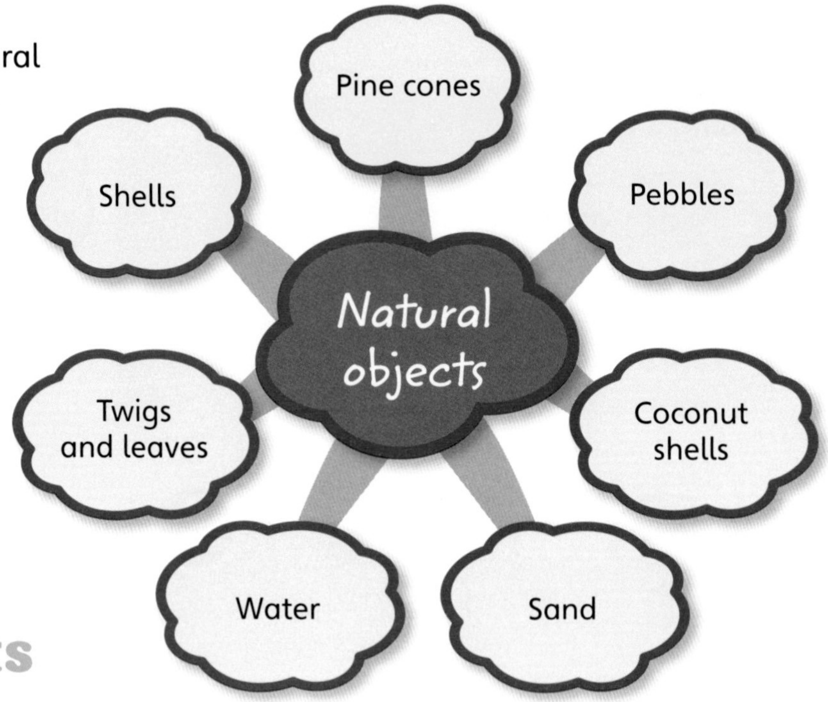

Choosing natural objects
- Make sure that all objects are clean.
- Check that they are not a choking hazard.
- Supervise children as they are playing with them.

Natural objects:
- Pine cones
- Shells
- Pebbles
- Twigs and leaves
- Coconut shells
- Water
- Sand

Natural environments

Children like playing outdoors. There are many places where children can play. Some settings take children out on trips to these places. It is always important to check that places outdoors are safe.

Say again?

Natural environment – this is another word for a place outdoors

Parks

Children like playing in parks. Parks may have trees and grassy areas.

Seaside

Some children are lucky to live near the seaside. There will be water and a beach.

Woods

Woods are great places for children. There are trees and leaves.

Gardens

Even small gardens have things for children to see and do. There may be hedges, trees or places to dig.

Developing children's curiosity

Outdoor experiences can develop children's curiosity. Let's look at the way that natural environments can help children's curiosity.

- **Parks** Children can look at trees and enjoy playing on the grass.
- **Seaside** Children can discover crabs, mussels and other creatures.
- **Woods** Children can look for squirrels and other animals. They can also see different leaves.
- **Gardens** Children can look for insects and notice birds.

See it, think it

What do you think these children are learning?

The local community

Within many communities there are places to go and things for children to do. These can help children to play or learn new skills.

Let's look at a few of the places in the community that can provide experiences for children.

Over to you...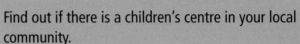

Find out if there is a children's centre in your local community.

Library

Libraries lend books. They also lend DVDs and have computers.

Toy library

A toy library lends toys and other resources for children and their families.

Swimming pool

Swimming pools give children and their families a chance to swim and play in water.

Sports centre

Sports centres allow children and their families to learn new sports and games. Some leisure centres have soft play areas for babies and toddlers.

Parent and toddler group

Parent and toddler groups can be found in many local communities. They allow parents and toddlers to join in activities with other families.

Children's centre

Many communities will have children's centres. Many children's centres will have sessions for children and their families. Many of the sessions help parents to gain skills and to enjoy being with their children.

Museum

Many museums have things for children to look at and sometimes touch and feel.

Finding out about the local community

Adults need to find out what there is for children in the local area. It can mean that children can try out new sports, games or equipment. It may also give children new play and learning experiences. It can help older children to make new friends.

Finding out about experiences for children

High five

1. Visit your local library.
2. Look in local newspapers.
3. Look in your local phone book.
4. Use the Internet.
5. Ask other people with children.

Ways to broaden children's experiences

Libraries

Most libraries provide advice about choosing books and DVDs. Many **librarians** will also run story and rhyme sessions for children.

Say again?

Librarian – this is the word for people who work in libraries

Toy library

Toy libraries often have times when children and families can stay and play with toys. They can provide advice about toys.

Swimming teacher

Swimming teachers help children learn to swim. This helps children to develop muscles and co-ordination.

Sports instructors

Sport instructors offer classes to help young children learn physical skills.

Parent and toddler groups

Parent and toddler groups can give children opportunities to play with new toys and have new experiences.

Museums

Museums often have special sessions for children. They may show children objects and let them dress up.

Children's centres

Some children's centres will have sessions for children and their families. These may include story sessions, baby massage classes as well as music sessions.

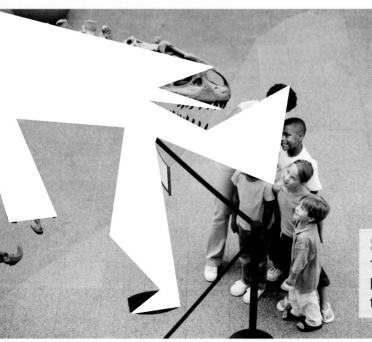

See it, think it
These children are at a museum. They are looking at a dinosaur skeleton. What do you think they might be learning?

Activity centre 14

1. Agony page AC 1.1

Can you explain to Ally how his son has learned what to do with cigarettes?

> I am a smoker. I am trying to stop. My son is 3 years old. Yesterday, he found a packet of cigarettes in my bag. He took one out and put it in his mouth. He looked as if he were smoking. Why did he do this?
>
> Ally

2. Case study AC 1.1, 1.2, 1.3

> Junaid is 3 years old. At nursery he is very busy. The nursery lets children explore and investigate. He enjoys playing with water. After story time, he often sits and looks at books, just like the adults. He also likes going into the garden and digging in the sand.

1. How is this child learning?

2. What learning is taking place?

3. Do it! AC 2.1

Go to your local library. Look at the books for children. Can you find a book for a baby, a toddler and a young child?

4. Agony page AC 3.1, 3.2, 3.3

Explain to this parent that her daughter can learn by playing outdoors and with natural objects.

> We live near a park. We do not have much money. Can my daughter still learn if she does not have many toys? She does play with things that she finds in the park.
>
> Tasha

5. Do it! AC 4.1, 4.3

Find out what there is for children in your local area. Find out what they do and think about why this would be good for children.

6. Do it! AC 2.2

Children like being involved in stories. Make some cards that have pictures that link to one of these stories:

The Gingerbread Man
Three Billy Goats Gruff
Goldilocks and the Three Bears

9. Odd one out! AC 2.3

All but one of these are ways to help children take part in stories and rhymes. Which is the odd one out?

Tell children to sit still and not move.
Let children hold the book.
Let children choose the rhymes.
Choose rhymes that have actions.

7. Agony page AC 4.2

Explain why this person should find out about what is going on in her local area.

> I have a 2 year old. Sometimes she gets bored. We do not have a garden. We are not near a park. We live in the city. I do not have money for toys. What should I do?
>
> Meena

10. Match up AC 3.3

Match the photographs to the sentences.

In the garden, children can look for insects.
In the woods, children can look at leaves.
At the seaside, children can play in sand.

8. Do it! AC 3.2

Make a collage that shows photographs of different natural environments.

How babies' development is supported by play (1)

Babies love to play. They need adults to play with them. On the next four pages we look at how play can help their development.

Let's start with babies' physical development.

Physical development

Hand movements

Babies need to learn to control their hands. Many play activities will help babies to use their hands while having fun. They might reach out for a rattle or try and push a button on a pop-up toy.

Large movements

Babies have to learn to get control of their arms and legs. Some play activities and toys can help them move their body. They may sit up when in a baby swing or use their legs when on a sit-and-ride toy.

Social and emotional development

Play can really help a baby to make strong relationships with adults. Play also helps parents and other special adults to make strong relationships with the baby.

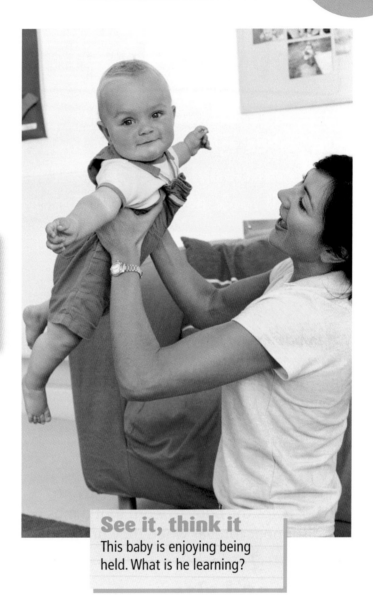

See it, think it
This baby is enjoying being held. What is he learning?

> ## Say again ?
>
> **Social and emotional development** – this is the way that babies learn to feel comfortable with others (it is also about their feelings)

Learning to trust

Babies need adults to play with them. Many games help the baby to trust them.

Making eye contact

Adults and babies will look at each other while they are playing. Learning to make this eye contact is important for their social skills.

Taking part

When babies are playing with adults, they are learning to take part. This is a social skill.

Learning to love

Playing with a baby takes time. Time spent with an adult helps babies to develop a special relationship with them.

How babies' development is supported by play (2)

On pages 132 and 133 we looked at how babies' physical, social and emotional development is supported by play. On this page, we will look at their intellectual and language development.

Intellectual development

When babies play they need to think. They also use their memories. This is why a baby will start to smile or join in when they see a familiar toy.

Thinking

Some play helps a baby to think. Playing 'peepo' helps the baby to learn that things do not disappear forever when they are hidden.

Shape and size

Some play helps babies to work out shapes and sizes. They may find that some things do not fit inside others.

Spot it
Can you see that this baby is learning about size and shape?

Say again?

Intellectual development – this is about the way babies and children learn to think and remember

Language development

In the first year of life, babies need to learn the sounds of language. They will do this by being with an adult. Playing is a good way of helping babies to hear speech. If an adult uses the same words and phrases each time they play with a baby, the baby will quickly remember the sounds.

Hearing the words

Adults are likely to talk as they are playing with babies. This means that babies are hearing the sound of words.

Recognising words

At around 7 months, babies start to work out that words have meanings. If adults use the same words when they play with a baby, the baby will start to understand the meaning of the words.

Enjoying books

Babies can learn to love books very early. Experts say that you should show books to babies.

Supporting babies' individual needs

Play can help babies' individual needs. To do this adults have to be good at understanding what a baby needs. Being rocked might comfort a baby who cries a lot. Playing 'peepo' might help a baby who needs to learn that things don't disappear forever. A baby who needs help with hand movements might be given things that are easy to grip.

Top tips

For helping language

- Make eye contact with babies.
- Point and name toys that you are using.
- Repeat actions while talking.
- Smile and make sure that games are fun.

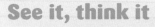

See it, think it

This baby is learning to walk. How is this play helping to support her needs?

We have seen that play is important for babies. Over the next eight pages, we will look at play activities for babies of different ages. We will also look at why these play activities and resources are good for babies.

Let's begin with babies aged from birth to 3 months.

Meeting babies' play needs: 0 to 3 months

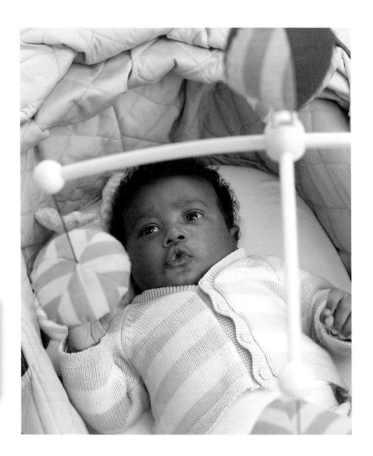

Very young babies need plenty of time with adults. They need to be held. They also need play activities and **resources** that help them to move their bodies.

Say again?

Resources – these are things such as toys that you might put out

Rattles

Rattles help young babies to turn towards sound. They also help them reach out and grasp. This will help their hand skills

Over to you...

Visit a toy shop. Look at the toys for babies aged 0 to 3 months. What do they do?

Mobiles

Mobiles can be soothing for young babies. They also help the baby to focus.

Musical toys

Toys that make sounds are soothing. They also help the baby to learn and listen to sounds.

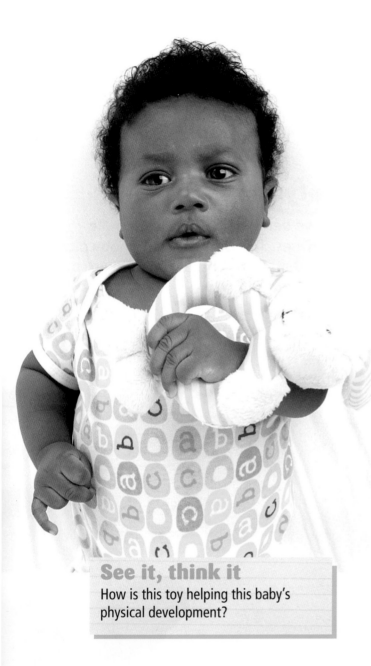

Hand-held toys

Babies like the feel of toys. Hand-held toys might be soft and cuddly. Some toys might make sounds.

Bath time

By the time babies are about 3 months old, most of them like bath time. It is a time when they can kick and splash. This is a good play activity, but you must never leave a baby alone in water. Also make sure that the water is not hot before putting the baby in.

Keeping babies safe **High five**

1. Do not leave babies alone with toys.
2. Make sure that toys are right for the age of the baby.
3. Check that toys are clean.
4. Check that toys are not broken.
5. Keep mobiles out of babies' reach.

See it, think it
How is this toy helping this baby's physical development?

Play activities and resources (2)

Babies grow quickly. They develop quickly. This means that we need to think about different play activities and resources.

Meeting babies' play needs: 4 to 7 months

Most babies at 4 months are starting to control their hands more. They like spending a little time on the floor. Many babies will start to roll over. Babies still need adults to play with them. Babies will explore items by putting them in their mouths. This means that we have to check that items are safe.

Baby mat

This is put on the floor. Babies can touch different textures. They can press buttons and make sounds. Baby mats help babies to use their hands. They also help babies to strengthen their back and head.

Baby gym

This is put on the floor. The baby lies on his or her back. This lets the baby kick and move his arms and helps to build muscles. It helps the baby to get more control.

Humpty Dumpty

Babies love being held. They like simple action rhymes. This game lets the baby play with the adult. It also helps the baby to balance and to sit up.

See it, think it
This adult is playing Humpty Dumpty. What is the baby learning?

Humpty Dumpty

- Sit the baby down on your lap, facing you.
- Hold the baby gently, but securely.
- Sing the rhyme while gently bouncing the baby up and down.
- On the line 'Humpty Dumpty had a great fall', open your knees slightly. This means that the baby will slip down just a little. Do make sure that the baby can feel that you are holding them safely.
- Put the baby back on to your knees again and finish the rhyme.

Choosing safe objects for babies

- Check that there are no loose parts.
- Make sure that it is too big for the baby to swallow.
- Make sure that it is too big for a baby to choke on.
- Make sure that it has no rough edges.

Over to you...

Look at a baby who is aged between 4 and 7 months. See what they like to hold. See how they put everything in their mouth.

Bath time and a rubber duck

Babies still love bath time. Babies can now enjoy toys in the bath. Many will like holding and sucking a rubber duck.

Spoons

Babies like feeling and mouthing objects. You can use household objects such as spoons for babies. You must choose hard objects and also things that are clean.

Babies from 8 months are starting to sit up. Some will also start to crawl. This means that they start to play differently. Let's look at what play activities and resources we can use.

Meeting babies' play needs: 8 to 11 months

Babies will still be putting things in their mouths. This means that things need to be safe. They are also starting to sit up and move. They also like exploring.

Pop-up toys

These toys are fun for babies. They like pressing buttons or turning knobs. This helps their hand movements.

See it, think it
What other things could be used in treasure basket play?

Treasure basket play

Treasure baskets are collections of safe objects from around the home. All the objects are made from natural things, such as a wooden spoon, a small metal bowl, a wooden peg, a leather purse. These objects help babies to touch and mouth. They also help babies' hand movements. They also help babies to learn about shape and size.

Items for treasure basket play

High five

1. Metal teaspoon
2. Cotton scarf
3. Real lemon (washed)
4. Metal scoop
5. Biscuit tin (empty!)

Baby books

Babies love books. This is a good age to introduce books. Books help babies to communicate. They also help babies to use their hands. If babies are shown the same book many times, they will start to recognise pictures.

Knock-down play

Babies love knocking down things. Babies' arm movements are helped as they reach out. Knock-down play also helps with co-ordination. Babies can learn about what happens when things fall down.

Play activities and resources (4)

At 12 months most babies are mobile. Many will start to walk. This means that they can do more. They also have more control over their hands. Let's see what play activities and resources we can use with them.

Meeting babies' play needs: 12 to 15 months

Babies will still be mouthing at this age, but will start to spend longer touching and feeling things. They will want to move around. They also like copying adults.

Sit-and-ride toys

Now babies can move, they like climbing and getting on things. Sit-and-ride toys help babies to balance. They also teach them new skills.

Stacking beakers

Babies like playing with stacking beakers. They can put them inside each other or they can make a tower with them. They can also put items inside them. They help babies' hand movements and co-ordination. They also help the baby learn about shape and size.

Balls

Babies like balls. Games where you roll a ball to a baby work well. The baby may roll it back or pick it up. They help the baby's hand movements. They also help the baby to learn to take turns.

Brick trolley

Babies like to push things. Brick trolleys are popular. They help babies to stand up and walk and to control their movements.

Spot it
Can you spot the skills that this baby is learning?

Keeping babies safe — High five

1. Do not leave babies alone.
2. Keep hot drinks away from babies.
3. Only give toys that are right for babies.
4. Make sure that electrical items are not in reach.
5. Use safety equipment (look at pages 73 and 78–79).

The table below shows the benefits of play activities for babies.

Age	Activity, game or toy	Benefits for the baby
0–3 months	Rattle	Helps hand skills
	Mobile	Helps the baby to focus
	Musical toy	Helps the baby to listen to sounds
	Hand-held toy	Helps hand skills
4–7 months	Bath time	Helps leg and arm muscles
	Baby mat	Helps hand skills Helps to strengthen back and head
	Baby gym	Helps to build muscles Helps the baby to get more control
	Humpty Dumpty	Lets the baby play with the adult Helps the baby to balance Helps the baby to sit up
	Bath time and a rubber duck	Helps the baby reach out Helps to strengthen arms and legs
	Spoon	Helps the baby to explore objects safely
8–II months	Pop-up toy	Helps hand movements
	Treasure basket play	Helps the baby to touch and mouth Helps the baby's hand movements Helps the baby to learn about shape and size
	Baby book	Helps the baby to communicate Helps babies to use their hands
	Knock-down play	Helps arm movements Helps co-ordination Helps the baby learn about what happens when objects fall
12–I5 months	Brick trolley	Helps the baby to stand up and walk Helps the baby to control its movements
	Stacking beaker	Helps hand movements and co-ordination Helps the baby learn about shape and size
	Ball	Helps hand movements Helps the baby to learn to take turns
	Sit-and-ride toy	Helps the baby to balance

The role of the adult

Babies need adults. They need adults to play with. They also need adults to keep them safe.

Following instructions

Most toys will have instructions about how to use them. They will also tell you what age they are for. You should only give babies toys that are meant for them.

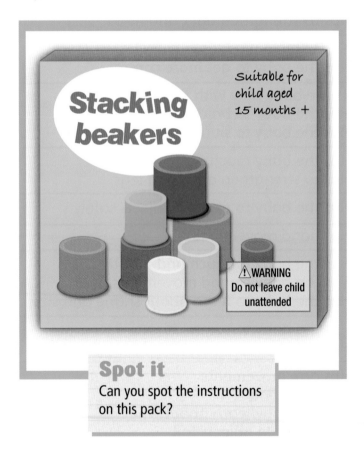

Stacking beakers

Suitable for child aged 15 months +

⚠ WARNING
Do not leave child unattended

Spot it
Can you spot the instructions on this pack?

Water

Babies love playing with water. But water can also be dangerous. Always check that water is not hot (36–38°C). A baby's skin burns very easily so water has to be just warm. You should never leave a baby alone with water.

Cleanliness

All babies put things in their mouths. It is their way of exploring. You cannot stop this. You can also make sure that everything is clean.

Choking

Babies can choke on small things. Make sure that everything you give a baby is too large for them to choke on it – the width of three adult fingers is about right.

Strangulation

Objects that we give to babies must not fit around their neck. This means that you need to watch out for lengths of ribbons or chains.

Supervision

Adults have to stay with babies all the time. This is because babies have no sense of danger. Even tiny babies can reach out and knock things over.

Falls

Babies can fall. This means that if you use swings, rockers or sit-and-ride toys, you must stay near babies. You should also not leave babies alone in highchairs.

How adults can help babies to play

Playing with babies is important. Babies need us to be their play partners. They can learn what to do and how to play from us. Let's look at some ways to play!

Smiling

Babies need to have fun. Smiling when you play with them can help play to be fun.

Making eye contact

Babies need us to make eye contact. This shows we are interested. It also helps them to communicate.

Talking to the baby

When we are playing, we need to talk to the baby. We may repeat words as we are repeating actions. This helps the baby learn to talk. We can also point out things for the baby.

Showing the baby what to do

There are times when we need to show babies what to do. We might shake a rattle or press a button on a toy.

Be ready to repeat play

Babies often need to repeat play over and over again. If they are happy, we need to keep joining in.

Guess what!

Babies are quick to copy the actions of adults.

Activity centre 15

1. Do it!
AC 1.1

Make a poster that shows parents how play can help babies' development. Try and use plenty of pictures.

2. Agony page
AC 1.1, 3.2

Read Ash's letter. Explain why play is good for babies. Give some ideas as to how she might play with her baby.

My baby is 6 months old. My mum says I should play with her. I cannot see the point. Isn't she too young?

Ash

4. Match up
AC 2.1

Look at these toys. Match up the toys to the age groups.

Baby 0–3 months
Baby 4–7 months
Baby 7–11 months
Baby 12–15 months

3. Do it!
AC 2.1, 2.2

Make a list of six toys and play activities that parents can use with their babies. Give reasons why these toys and play activities are good for babies.

5. Odd one out!   AC 2.2

All but one of these will help babies to use their legs. Which is the odd one out?

Baby book
Baby gym
Bath time
Sit-and-ride toys

7. True or false?   AC 3.I

Are these statements true or false when choosing toys for babies?

	True	False
Check that they are right for their age.	☐	☐
Check that they make noises.	☐	☐
Check that they are clean.	☐	☐
Check that they are not broken.	☐	☐
Check that they are bright.	☐	☐

6. Match up   AC 2.2

Look at the toys and activities. Match up the toys and activities to the sentences.

It helps babies to kick and splash in the bath.
It helps babies to feel objects and shapes.
It helps babies to balance.
It helps babies to control their hands.

8. Do it!   AC 3.2

Make a poster that shows adults how best to play with babies.

Features of a positive learning environment (1)

Children learn best through play. Adults working with children have to create places where they can play and learn.

Let's look at some of the things that we might find in a **positive learning environment**.

Say again?

Positive learning environment – a place that has everything set up so that children can happily learn while playing

Toys

The toys that are put out for children have to be interesting. They also need to be right for children's age or stage of development. A pop-up toy might be right for a baby, but would quickly become boring for a 4 year old. Below are some examples of toys for children aged from 2 years.

Small world play

Trains, farm animals and play people.

Construction sets

Duplo®, Lego®, wooden blocks.

Toys for pretend play

Cookers, telephones, cash tills

Why toys will help children to learn

Toys can help children to learn. Toys can encourage children's imagination and also skills. Choosing toys that are right for children is a skill.

Find out!

Do you remember the toys that you could give to babies?

Look at page 143.

Choosing toys   High five

1. Check that toys are safe.
2. Check that toys are right for age/stage.
3. Put out some toys that children have not seen for a while.
4. Work out which toys children enjoy most.
5. Put out toys alongside other resources.

Resources and materials

As well as toys, children like to play with other things. Let's look at some very popular materials and resources. Many settings will often put out different resources and toys together, such as sand and toy dinosaurs.

Why resources help children to learn

Resources and materials help children to use their hands. They also help children to use their imagination. Children can do new things with them.

Layout

The way that resources and toys are put out is important. Some toys and resources are best on the floor. Others are best on a table. A good layout makes it easy for children to get things out and put them away.

Dough

Water

Sand

Resources

Collage materials

Junk modelling materials

Paint

Why layout helps children to learn

A good layout makes it easy for children to play. They do not have to keep asking adults for help. Getting things out and putting them away helps children to feel confident. A good layout also prevents accidents. Children do not get in each other's way.

See it, think it
These children are happily playing. What do you think they are learning?

Features of a positive learning environment (2)

We saw on pages 148 and 149 that toys, resources and layout are important. But there are other things as well. These are about children feeling cared for, comfortable and safe.

Feeling cared for

Many young children are often away from their parents when they are in settings. It is important that they feel cared for and loved. Most children will have a **key person** who will take special care of them. This will help children to settle in and feel comfortable. There are other things that help children feel cared for and special. Let's look at a few:

- names on pegs
- resources that reflect children's home culture
- adults who are interested in and listen to children.

Say again ?

Key person – this is someone who takes special care of a child when their parents are not there

Key person   High five

1. A key person helps children to settle in.
2. A key person gets to know the child.
3. A key person gets to know the family.
4. A key person takes a special interest in the child.
5. A key person is there for the child whenever they need someone.

Why feeling cared for helps children to learn

Children who are totally happy can play easily. They can relax and they can concentrate. It is important for children to feel that they belong. Seeing things that remind you of home can help children feel wanted.

See it, think it

This child is with their key person. Why might this help the child to feel cared for?

Comfortable environment

Children play well when they are comfortable. There are many ways to make children feel comfortable.

Why feeling comfortable helps children to learn

It is hard to play and learn if you are hungry, cold or thirsty. Children need to have their basic needs met before they can play well. Children also relax more in environments that seem comfortable and bright.

Comfortable environment
- Right clothing for weather
- Right temperature in room
- Rugs, cushions and carpets
- Right furniture to meet children's needs
- Food and water to meet children's individual needs
- Good lighting
- Interesting displays

Clean and safe

A positive learning environment is clean and safe. It means that children can get on and play without any danger. Let's look at some things that are important.

Why being safe helps children to learn

Keeping the environment clean and safe stops children from becoming ill. It stops children from having accidents. Feeling ill stops children from playing. Accidents also stop children from playing.

Clean and Safe
- Clean toys and resources
- Safe toys and resources
- Personal hygiene routines, e.g. washing hands after going to toilet
- Clean floors, toilets and kitchen areas
- Safety equipment used, e.g. door and window locks, safety gates

How play helps children's physical development

Children learn through play. Their development can also be helped through play. Over the next few pages, we will look at how play can help children.

Let's start with **physical development**.

How play can help children's hand movements

We need our hands to help us hold things and to carry out many little jobs, such as dressing, cooking and feeding. Play can encourage children to use their hands and to develop skills. Let's look at some examples.

Dough

Young children like playing with dough. Dough can help children to use their hands in different ways. They may roll out the dough. They may cut it.

Water

Young children like playing with water. They may pour it. They may push things down into it. They may pour water into funnels.

Bricks

Playing with bricks requires a lot of skill. Children have to use their hands to put bricks on top of each other.

Spot it
Can you spot how this child is using her hands?

How play can help children to move

Some games and play help children to move. Moving strengthens children's legs. Moving helps their co-ordination and balance. Moving around also helps children to stay healthy. Let's look at some play that encourages movement.

Scooters

These little scooters make children move around. They strengthen children's leg muscles.

Climbing frame

Climbing helps children's co-ordination. It helps strengthen the arms and the legs.

Hide and seek

This game is fun for children. They have to run off in order to hide. This game helps them to keep fit.

Swings

Most children love being in a swing. Babies and toddlers learn to balance as the swing moves. Older children learn to use their legs to make the swing move.

See it, think it

This child is having fun playing. How is this play helping his physical development?

How play helps children's social and emotional development

Children can gain many social skills through play. These begin when children are babies. Play can also help children express their emotions.

Let's look at how play can help children's **social development**.

Enjoying being with others

It is important that children enjoy being with others. Play is a good way for children to enjoy being with other children. Most children start to do this well from the age of 3 years. Babies and toddlers learn to enjoy playing with adults.

Peepo

This simple game helps babies to have fun while making eye contact with adults.

Building a den

Children enjoy making things together. A den made from fabric and boxes helps children have fun together.

Parachute games

Parachute games are great fun for children. Adults help children to play alongside each other.

Spot it
Can you spot how these children are having fun together?

Taking turns

Taking turns can be hard for young children. From the age of 3 years most children start to take turns. Games and play can help children learn to take turns.

Slide

Children have to learn to take their turn on the slide. Young children often need an adult to remind them.

How play supports children's emotional development

Play also supports children's **emotional development**. It can help children express their emotions. It also helps them to learn about other people's feelings.

Expressing feelings

There are many ways in which children can express their feelings. Play should be fun for children. It can also help children sort out how they are feeling. Let's look at some ways.

> **Say again?**
>
> **Emotional development** – this is about children's feelings

See it, think it
This girl is pretending to be angry?
How is she learning about emotions?

Paint

Children enjoy painting. They also use painting as a way of showing that they are angry, sad or happy.

Dough

Dough often helps children who are frustrated. They can pinch and squash it. This helps them to feel better. Children also enjoy making things. This gives them confidence.

Musical instruments

There is something satisfying about making a noise. Children can be noisy or quiet when they are making sounds. Children also gain confidence from exploring sounds.

Understanding other people's feelings

Through play, children learn about other's feelings. We are likely to see children using small world play or pretend play to do this.

Small world play

Small world play uses objects like dinosaurs, farm animals and play people.

Children often make their own little worlds with these. They often act out the part of 'adult'. They tell the characters what they can and cannot do.

> **Examples of small world play**   **High five**
> 1. Farm animals
> 2. Cars
> 3. Play people
> 4. Dinosaurs
> 5. Train set

How play helps children's intellectual development

Children can learn and think about many things as they are playing. Play needs to be challenging and interesting.

Let's look at how play supports children's **intellectual development**.

How play can help children's memory

Some types of play can help children's memory. Let's look at a few popular ones.

Pairs

This is a game where children have to match pictures. It can help children learn to remember.

Kim's game

This is a game in which objects are put on to a tray. The adult takes away an object. The children have to work out what is missing.

How play can help children's problem solving

Some types of play can help children to work out things. Here are a few types of play that can be used.

Construction play

This is where children are making things. They may use wooden blocks, bricks or Duplo®, Lego®.

Making dens

This can help children to work together, and also helps them to solve problems. They have to think about shape and size.

Shape sorters

Toddlers often enjoy playing with shape sorters. They have to look at shapes and decide where to put them. At first adults may need to help toddlers with this type of play.

How play helps children to learn concepts

There are many **concepts** that children need to learn. These include shape, size and measurements. They also can learn about colour. Children can learn through play.

Say again ?

Concepts – these are general ideas that children have to learn such as colour or time

Spot it
Can you spot how this child is learning about measuring?

Jigsaws

These help children to think about shape. At first children need adults to help them.

Water and sand

Playing in water and sand can help children learn about measuring. They often like pouring and filling containers.

Climbing frame

When children are climbing, they are exploring shape and space. They do this by moving their arms and legs into places.

Top tips

Helping children's intellectual development

- Play alongside children.
- Talk to children about what they are doing.
- Explain to children why things happen, for example 'this is not sinking because there is air in it'.
- Play games that help children to think and remember, such as Snap and Happy Families.

How play helps children's language development

Talking and listening are important skills for children to learn. They also have to learn how to talk to express their feelings and ideas. Play can help children do this. Let's see how.

How play helps children to talk

Some types of play can help children to talk. Sometimes this is because children want to talk to adults about what they are doing. Sometimes this is because children want to talk to each other.

Playing with telephones

Toddlers love chatting away on a play phone. Older children also like to talk as part of their pretend play.

Puppets

Children often talk if an adult uses a puppet. Children ask the puppet questions. They like to tell the puppet things.

Play people

When children play with small world objects such as play people, they often talk. They often tell the play people what to do.

See it, think it
This child is chatting away on the play phone. How is this helping his speech?

How play helps children to listen

Play can also help children to listen. There are games that they can play. They also learn to listen by playing with other children.

Sound lotto

This is a game where children listen to sounds. They have to match the sound to a picture. It works well with children from 3 years old.

Action rhymes

Rhymes with actions such as Humpty Dumpty help babies and toddlers to listen. Babies and toddlers need an adult to help them.

Pretend play

From around the age of 3 years children love playing with each other. They love dressing up and talk a lot together. This helps children to talk and to listen.

How play helps children to enjoy early writing

Young children often write by making marks. This helps their handwriting. It also helps them to enjoy writing.

How play helps children to enjoy reading

Young children do not begin learning to read until they are at school. They can learn a lot about reading and books before this. They can do this through play.

Story sacks

These are bags that have a book in them. They also have some play props. With an adult, the child can take part in the story.

Spot it

Can you spot how this child is enjoying writing?

Language development and play **High five**

1. Put out paper and pens in different play areas.
2. Change the home corner so that children have new things to talk about.
3. Use a lot of action nursery rhymes with children of all ages.
4. Play sound games to encourage children's listening skills.
5. Use puppets to encourage children to talk.

How play should meet children's needs

Adults have to make sure that all children can play. There are many ways of doing this. Let's look at a few.

Understanding children's needs

Some children have particular needs. They may not see well or they may not be able to hold things easily. Some children have learning difficulties. It is important to understand children's needs. Parents might tell us what their child needs. Once we understand the needs, then we can meet them. Here are some examples.

| Child who has sight problems | → | • Bright toys
• Good light in room
• Keep room tidy |

| Child who has mobility needs | → | • Put toys at a good height for the child
• Think about layout |

| Child who has learning needs | → | • Choose toys that interest the child
• Make sure that the toys are right for stage of development |

| Child new to the setting | → | • Play with adult
• Games to help the child play with other children |

How resources might support or challenge stereotyping or discrimination

When we put out toys or resources for children, we need to make sure that they are right. Some toys or resources might help children but some might give them the wrong idea about other people. Let's look at this a little more.

Say again?

Stereotype – an idea that people have about a group of people which might not be true
Discrimination – this is about the way that a group might not be treated fairly

Toys and resources that challenge stereotyping or discrimination

Adults must think about how toys and resources help children to feel positively about others. Let's look at ways to do this.

Home corner ✔

We can put items in the home corner. We can choose things that help children learn that some people may cook differently. We can choose things that help children learn that other families might like different things.

Books and posters ✔

We can put items out which show positive images that reflect our multicultural society. We may put up posters that welcome everyone in a range of languages.

Dolls ✔

We can put out dolls that represent a range of different races. It is important that these are attractive. Adults must show children how to play with them nicely.

Toys and resources that reinforce stereotyping and discrimination

Children can pick up ideas about other people from things that they play with. Adults need to look at what they put out for the children. They also need to look at the way that children are playing with things.

Boys' or girls' toys ✗

It is good to make sure that all children get a chance to play. Toys that are only blue or only pink can stop children from playing with them.

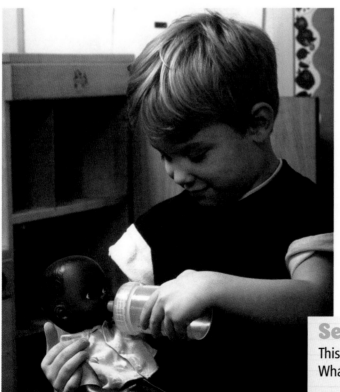

Challenging discrimination

High five

1. Look for resources that show children from around the world.
2. Make sure that images of others are positive.
3. Make sure that resources showing different cultures and religions are used correctly.
4. Make sure that adults keep resources from different cultures and religions nicely.
5. Look for resources that both boys and girls will enjoy using.

See it, think it
This boy is enjoying playing with this doll. What positive learning is taking place?

Activity centre 16

1. Match up
AC 1.1, 1.2

Can you match up these photos with the statements about features of a positive learning environment?

Children's needs are met so that they are comfortable.

Toys that are right for children's age and stage are available.

Interesting materials are available to play with.

Children are kept safe.

2. Odd one out!
AC 1.1

All but one of these are features of a positive learning environment. Which is the odd one out?

Walls are blue and red

Children are kept safe

Resources are right for children's needs

3. Do it! AC 1.1

Visit a pre-school, nursery or childminder's. Make a list of features that help children to:

- feel comfortable
- stay safe
- feel cared for
- play and learn.

5. Agony page AC2.1

Tell Danni how play can help children's physical and intellectual development. Give some examples of toys and games.

I want to work in a nursery. During the interview I have to talk about how play helps children's physical and intellectual development.

Danni

4. Match up AC 2.1

Match the play up to the areas of development that it might cover. The first one has been done as an example.

Rolling out dough	→	Physical
Scooping sand		
		Intellectual
Using a shape sorter with an adult		Social
Using a climbing frame		Emotional
Dressing up play with others		Language

6. Do it! AC 3.1

Look at some children's books. Find some books that have positive images of a range of different people.

8

Activities
for children

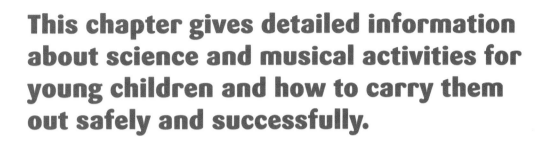

This chapter gives detailed information about science and musical activities for young children and how to carry them out safely and successfully.

The units covered in this chapter are:

CFC21 Science activities for young children
CFC23 Musical activities for young children

In this chapter you will learn about:

- science activities suitable for children aged 18 months to 2 years, and 3 years to 5 years
- the resources needed to carry out the science activity for children aged 18 months to 2 years, and 3 years to 5 years
- the possible health and safety risks of science activities
- the support a child may need when carrying out science activities and what a child would be expected to learn
- musical activities suitable for babies under 6 months, young children 1 to 2 years and young children 3 to 5 years
- the benefits to the child of musical activities
- how to make musical activities and games for young children
- the value to young children of musical activities and games and the learning that could take place.

Science activities

Children are naturally curious. They like exploring. They also notice things. These are all important when it comes to science.

Concept	What children might learn
Speed	How things move – what makes things move faster
Water	How water changes with heat How things float, sink or submerge when in water
Textures and properties of materials and objects	How things can feel different How things can stretch How things can be stuck together How things can be mixed together
Heat	How heat can change things – cooking
Light	How mirrors reflect images How magnifying sheets make things larger
Electricity	How things are powered Why batteries are needed in some things
Colour	How paint colours change when they are mixed
Air	How to make bubbles How things move in the wind
Magnetism	How magnets attract or repel
Weather	How the weather changes Temperature
Sound	How things make sounds

There are plenty of activities that are fun for children, but also help them explore scientific concepts. Let's look at the type of things that children might learn.

See it, think it
This child is playing with magnetic toys. What might he be learning?

At what age can children do science activities?

Children are learning about the world around them all the time. A science activity for young children is about doing and seeing things. It is not about explaining 'why' things happen. They will learn this later on.

Activities for children aged 18 months to 2 years

Toddlers need activities that keep them busy. They also like touching things with their hands. Below are some examples of activities that work well with toddlers.

- Making stretchy dough
- Playing with magnetic toys
- Mixing paint colours
- Science activities: 3 to 5 years
- Putting batteries in a torch
- Making a boat for teddy
- Making a marble run

- Catching bubbles
- Gloop (cornflour and water mix)
- Ice cubes in water
- Science activities: 18 months to 2 years
- Posting objects down large tubes
- Musical instruments
- Looking through magnifying sheets

Activities for children aged 3 to 5 years

From the age of 3 years, children can talk more about what they are doing. They also have more control over their hands. They are less likely to put things in their mouths. This means that we can add in some more activities.

Choosing science activities **High five**

1. Look for things that children can do easily.
2. Make sure that items are safe.
3. Think about the age/stage of development.
4. Work out what children might learn.
5. Think about how much supervision is required.

A science activity for children aged 18 months to 2 years

There are many activities that we can do with toddlers. Let's look at some.

Ice cubes in water

Young children love playing with water. Ice cubes can be put in a washing up bowl of water. The children can touch and explore them.

Resources

You will need:

- a tray of ice cubes
- washing up bowl
- cloth to wipe up spills
- aprons.

How activities will help children to learn

Let's look at the way that the activities in the table below might help children to learn.

Activity	What children might learn
Ice cubes in water	That ice is cold That ice melts into water
Gloop (corn flour and water mix)	That gloop can be runny and solid
Catching bubbles	That bubbles pop when you touch them That bubbles fall to the ground
Posting objects down large tubes	That things reappear That round objects roll That objects roll faster if the tube is slanted
Looking through magnifying sheets	That objects appear larger when magnified
Musical instruments	That sound is made when you hit or shake instruments That sound is louder if you hit or shake instruments more

Spot it

Can you spot how this toddler is enjoying playing with the bubbles?

Health and safety for science activities with toddlers

- Toddlers like putting things in their mouths. Adults have to think about this when putting things out. You should not put out anything the toddler might choke on.
- Toddlers spill things. Adults have to be ready to wipe up spills to stop accidents.
- Toddlers can drown in only a little water. Any activities involving water need to be supervised.
- Toddlers find it hard to share. They may bite or scratch another child. Adults have to make sure that they put out enough things for toddlers. They must also supervise.

Supporting toddlers

Toddlers find it hard to follow instructions. Adults can support toddlers by showing them what to do. This way, toddlers can copy. Toddlers also need adults to talk to them. This helps them to learn the names of things.

A science activity for children aged 3 to 5 years

As children get older there are plenty of science activities for them to do. Let's look at one.

Making dough

Children love cooking. Making stretchy dough is easy for children. This type of dough does not need cooking. You just add a little food colouring into a jug of water. Then you mix a little water and a cup of self-raising flour together. (Note: This dough cannot be kept – it needs to be thrown away after the activity is finished.)

Resources

You will need:

- a mixing bowl for each child
- spoon for mixing
- self-raising flour
- food colouring
- water
- aprons
- cloth to wipe up spills.

See it, think it

These children are making dough. Why is it important that each child has their own dough?

Health and safety for science activities

- Some children are allergic to food and other things. Always make sure you know about any allergies before starting an activity.
- Children may become excited. Always supervise activities.
- Small items can be swallowed. Always supervise activities.
- Batteries can be poisonous. Supervise the activity.
- Children can drown in water. Always supervise activities.

Supporting children

Children need time in order to explore activities. If they are making things, they may also need step-by-step instructions. Children also need adults to talk to them so that they can learn about what they are seeing.

How activities will help children to learn

Let's look at the way that the activities on page 167 might help children to learn.

Activity	What children might learn
Making stretchy dough	That water and flour make a mixture That too much water will make a mixture sticky That leaving stretchy dough uncovered will make it dry
Playing with magnetic toys	That magnets try to come together That magnets will attract some other metal items
Mixing paint colours	That some colours when mixed make new colours That adding white to colours will make them paler
Making a marble run	That objects will roll quickly if they are put on a slope
Putting batteries in a torch	That some things need batteries to work That batteries need to be put in the right way
Making a boat for teddy	That some things float That some things are waterproof

Activity centre 17

1. Agony page

AC 1.1

My nursery says that I have to plan some science activities. I work with a 2 year old and a 4 year old. Help!

Cher

Tell Cher about some science activities she could do.

2. True or false?

AC 1.1

Tick which of these are good science activities for children aged 3–5 years.

	True	False
Mixing paint colours	☐	☐
Reading a book	☐	☐
Making a marble run	☐	☐
Watching television	☐	☐
Making stretchy dough	☐	☐

3. Do it!

AC 1.2, 2.1

Make a poster that shows a science activity for children 18 months–2 years and another for children aged 3–5 years. Make sure that your poster helps people to know what they will need.

4. True or false?

AC 2.2

Which of these statements are true and which are false?

	True	False
Toddlers might put things in their mouths.	☐	☐
You can leave children alone to play with water.	☐	☐
Toddlers find it hard to share.	☐	☐
Batteries can be poisonous.	☐	☐
Children are not allergic to flour.	☐	☐

5. Odd one out!   AC 2.3

All but one of these are ways of supporting a 2 year old during a science activity. Which is the odd one out?

Tell the child to be quiet
Show the child what to do
Encourage the child to explore

6. Do it!   AC 3.3

Make a poster that shows parents what children aged 18 months to 2 years might learn from:

- catching bubbles
- playing with ice cubes in water
- looking through a magnifying sheet.

7. Match up   AC 3.1

Match up the science activities to the learning

Children learn about melting.
Children learn about making sounds.
Children learn some things need batteries.
Children learn that some things float.

Musical activities for babies under 6 months

Young babies like music. They like rhythms. There are many activities that babies can enjoy.

Let's look at some musical activities that you can do with young babies.

Finger rhymes

These rhymes are fun because you use your fingers. Babies enjoy watching you. They also enjoy hearing words. Finger rhymes help babies to learn words. They also help babies learn to play.

Lullabies
'Bye Baby Bunting'

Simple musical instruments
Rattles and shakers

Musical activities for young babies

Finger rhymes
'Two little dicky birds'
'Pat-a-cake

Action rhymes
'Row, row, row the boat'
'Humpty Dumpty'

Action rhymes

These rhymes have actions. Babies soon learn what is about to happen. They start to recognise the words and the sounds. They will also try to join in with the actions. Doing these actions will help their bodies to develop.

See it, think it
This baby is hearing 'Row, row, row the boat'. What is the baby learning?

Lullabies

These are rhymes where adults sing and rock the baby. Babies are often calmed by these songs. They also enjoy being rocked. These rhymes help babies to learn words. They help babies to relax.

Simple musical instruments

Rattles and shakers help babies to make sounds. Babies learn to grasp and shake them. This is good for their hands. They also learn that different rattles make different sounds.

Carrying out musical activities with babies

High five

1. Don't worry if you are not good at singing.
2. Choose a time when the baby is not tired or hungry.
3. Learn the rhymes and actions first.
4. Make eye contact with the baby.
5. Expect to repeat the rhyme a couple of times before getting a reaction.

See it, think it

There are many different rattles and shakers. Why is it good for a baby to have a choice?

Musical activities for children aged 1 to 2 years

Toddlers love musical games and activities. They like making sounds. They like dancing.

Let's look at some activities for 1 to 2 year olds.

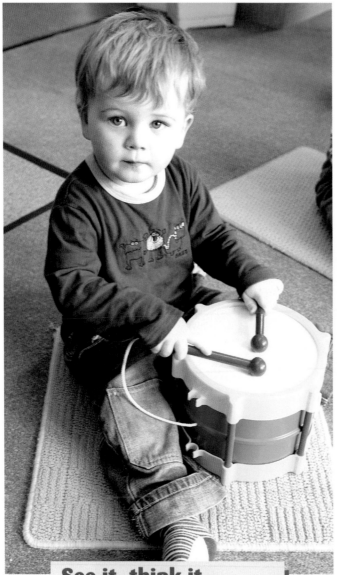

Rhymes and songs
'Hickory Dickory Dock'
'Diddle Diddle Dumpling'
'Three Blind Mice'

Musical activities 1 to 2 years

Simple musical instruments
Drums, rattles and shakers

Music for dancing
Dancing to CDs

Simple musical instruments

Toddlers love making noises. They enjoy hitting drums and using shakers. Musical instruments help toddlers to control their hands. They help them to learn how to make sounds. They help toddlers to join in with others.

See it, think it
This child is enjoying hitting the drum.
What skills is he learning?

Spot it

Can you spot how this toddler is joining in with the adult?

Rhymes and songs

Toddlers like all sorts of rhymes. Try out action rhymes and also finger rhymes. Look out for rhymes that they can join in with. Rhymes help toddlers to learn words. They help toddlers to make sounds.

Music for dancing

Toddlers enjoy dancing. They like moving to music in time with a beat. They like copying adults. Dancing helps toddlers to develop control of their bodies. It helps them to join in with adults.

Music with toddlers **High five**

1. Look out for music that has a simple beat.
2. Choose music carefully – no swearing in the words!
3. Dance with children.
4. Be ready to stop if toddlers have had enough.
5. Notice which music the toddlers like best.

Musical activities for children aged 3 to 5 years

Most young children love music. They love making music. They love moving to it.

Dancing
Dancing to music

Musical games
Musical statues
'Hokey Cokey'

Musical activities 3 to 5 years

Rhymes
'Ring a ring o' roses'
'I'm a little teapot'
'Hey Diddle, Diddle'

Musical instruments
Xylophones, drums, tambourines, shakers

Musical games

Musical games are fun for children. They learn how to play together. They learn to follow rules. They also learn the words of the songs and have fun.

Dancing

Children love moving to music. Dancing helps children's co-ordination. It helps children to express their emotions.

Rhymes

There are many rhymes that children can learn. Rhymes are good for children's speech. It helps them to hear sounds in words. This will help them later for reading. Counting rhymes help children learn numbers. Rhymes also help children to feel part of a group.

Musical instruments

Children like playing with musical instruments. They help children to gain control of their hands and express emotions. They help children to learn about making sounds.

Musical instruments — High five

1. Homemade shakers, such as plastic bottles with rice
2. Chime bars
3. Wooden sticks
4. Drums
5. Tambourines

See it, think it

These children are singing. What skills are they learning?

Musical activities and games for young children

Young children love simple musical activities and games. Let's look at some activities and games.

Hokey cokey

This is a lovely group activity. Children have fun copying and joining in. Children quickly learn the words.

Value for children

Children enjoy this game. They enjoy being with others. They enjoy making the movements.

What children might learn

Children learn to sing the words. They learn parts of the body and actions. They also learn to co-operate with other children.

Musical statues

This is a game where children have to stay still when they cannot hear music. When there is music they can run around. It is important that there is enough room for this activity.

What children might learn

Children learn to listen carefully to the music. It also helps them to control their bodies. This game also helps children to get exercise.

Value for children

Children enjoy this game. It helps them feel part of the group.

Head, shoulders, knees and toes

This is an activity that can be played with three or four children. Adults have to join in with the actions and singing.

Value for children

Children enjoy playing this game. They enjoy singing and making the actions.

What children might learn

From this game, children learn the names of parts of the body. They learn to listen carefully to the words. They are also learning to sing in tune.

Musical games **High five**

1. Make sure that games are right for children's age/stage.
2. Keep games simple.
3. Join in games with children.
4. Remember that children may need to play games several times before they work out what to do.
5. Be ready to stop if children are getting bored.

Activity centre 18

1. Match up   AC 1.1

Match the photographs to the sentences.

Babies enjoy playing with rattles.
Toddlers love dancing to music.
Young children love musical games.

2. Do it!   AC 1.1

Learn the words to three nursery rhymes.

3. Odd one out!   AC 1.1

All but one of these are suitable activities for a young baby aged 0–6 months.

Which is the odd one out?

Saying Pat-a cake to the baby.
Playing music so the baby can dance.
Showing the baby a rattle.

4. Do it!   AC 1.1

Make a poster that gives parents ideas for musical activities for babies and children. Use some pictures.

5. True or false? AC I.2

Benefits of nursery rhymes

Which of these statements are true and which are false?

	True	False
Rhymes can help babies' and children's speech.	☐	☐
Rhymes can stop babies from snoring.	☐	☐
Rhymes can help calm babies.	☐	☐
Rhymes can help children learn to count.	☐	☐
Rhymes are good to keep children still.	☐	☐

6. Agony page AC I.2

Explain to Carlie why she should carry on. Tell her why it is good for toddlers to hear rhymes and to dance.

I sing a lot of rhymes to my toddler. I also put on music and we dance together. My mates laugh at me. They say that it is too early to do this. What do you think?

Carlie

7. Do it! AC 2.I

Look up some musical games and activities. Learn how to play or do them. Try them out with some children.

8. True or false? AC 2.2, 2.3

Which of these statements are true and which are false?

	True	False
Children can learn to play with others.	☐	☐
It is a way of teaching children to be good.	☐	☐
Children can learn new words and actions.	☐	☐
Children will be able to play the piano.	☐	☐

9

Parenting

This chapter gives information about contraception, pregnancy and the responsibilities of new parents.

The units covered in this chapter are:

CFC8 Contraception information
CFC6 Responsibilities of new parent(s)

In this chapter you will learn about:

- methods of contraception
- the strengths and weaknesses of each method of contraception listed
- where support on contraception can be obtained
- professionals available to talk to individuals about contraception
- the stages of pregnancy from conception to birth
- how a mum-to-be should care for herself before the birth of her baby
- factors which could harm an unborn baby
- support that new parent(s) may need during the first 12 weeks of a baby's life
- where to obtain support for the new baby, the new mum, the new parent(s).

Methods of contraception

Having a baby is a big step. Many people are not ready for a baby. Using contraception can stop you from having a baby.

There are many different types of **contraception**. Let's look at some types.

Say again?

Contraception – this is about ways of not getting pregnant – some people call it birth control

Condoms

These are latex sheaths. They work by stopping a man's sperm from getting into the woman. They go over the man's penis.

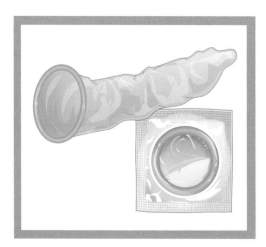

Strengths

- You can get them easily.
- They can also stop infections from being passed on.
- They work if used properly.

Weaknesses

- It can be embarrassing to stop and get one out.
- They can be fiddly to put on.
- They have to be put on correctly.

Contraceptive pill

These are tablets that a woman takes every day. They change the way a woman's body works. They stop it from producing eggs.

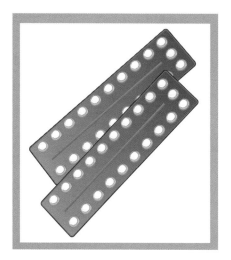

Strengths

- They work well if a woman takes them every day.

Weaknesses

- Some pills have to be taken at the same time every day in order to work.

- If women forget to take a pill every day or are late, it may not work.
- If a woman has been sick or is on antibiotics it might not work.
- It is a drug and has some side effects.
- You may not get the pill if you are a smoker.

Diaphragm (cap)

This goes inside the woman's vagina. It stops the sperm from moving up into the womb.

Strengths

- It can be put in before sex.
- It is not a drug.
- It has no side effects.

Weaknesses

- Women have to get fitted with the right size.
- It can take time to learn to use it.
- It does not work as well as the pill, patch or the condom.

Patch

A patch is put like a plaster on the skin, for example on the arm. The patch puts chemicals into the woman's body. It changes the way a woman's body works. It stops her from releasing eggs.

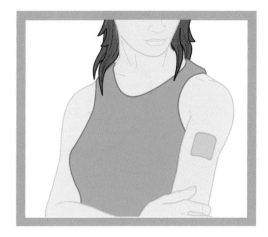

Strengths

- It works well.
- There is nothing to remember every day.

Weaknesses

- It is a drug and so has side effects.
- The patch can be seen.
- You may not get it if you are smoker.

Types of contraception — High five

1. There are many types of contraception.
2. Contraception only works if it is used properly.
3. Only condoms help stop infections from being passed on.
4. You can use more than one type of contraception at the same time, such as the condom and the pill.
5. You can get free contraception at a health centre.

Contraception advice

There are many types of contraception. It is important to find out what is best for you.

Let's look at where you can go to get contraception.

Youth services
You may need an appointment.

Sexual health clinic
You can often walk in.

Finding contraception

Contraceptive clinic
You can often walk in.

Chemist
You can walk in.

Family doctor (G.P.) or nurse
You will need an appointment.

Finding out about contraception

You can find out about clinics in your area by going into a chemist. You could also ask at a doctor's.

Getting advice — High five

1. Don't be worried – nurses and doctors are used to talking about sex.
2. Tell them everything – you can only get good help if you answer all the questions truthfully.
3. Follow their advice – contraception only works if you use it properly.
4. Remember to make an appointment if you go to your doctor's.
5. Ask whether you can get contraception for free.

People you can talk to

There are many people who can talk to you about contraception. They can give you advice. They can help you to choose what is right for you. What you say to these people is confidential. This means that they cannot tell other people.

Family doctor

They will know about any medical problems that you have. They are not allowed to tell anyone in your family that they have seen you.

Practice nurse

Most family doctors work in a building where there are nurses. Practice nurses can talk to you about contraception.

Pharmacist

Pharmacists can give you some advice. They can sell you condoms. They will tell you where to go for help.

Say again?

Pharmacist – this is someone who works in a chemist's and gets medicines ready

Contraception and sexual health nurses

These are nurses who can give out contraception. They can help you choose what is right for you. You can find them in sexual health clinics. Some may also come to colleges and schools.

I. Match up

AC I.I, I.2

Match up the drawings to the sentences.

It is good against infections.
These need to be taken each day.
It is like a plaster.
It needs to be the correct size.

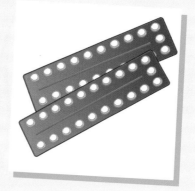

E3

2. True or false? AC 1.2

Are these statements about condoms true or false?

	True	False
They do not work.	☐	☐
They can stop infections.	☐	☐
They can prevent pregnancy.	☐	☐
They must be put on properly.	☐	☐
They can make you feel sick.	☐	☐

4. Odd one out! AC 2.1

All but one of these are places to go to get advice about contraception. Which is the odd one out?

The sexual health clinic
The chemist
The dentist
The doctor

3. Agony page AC 1.1, 2.2

Tell Kerry how she could be in charge of the contraception. Tell her where she should go to get help.

> I don't want to get pregnant. My boyfriend will not use a condom. What could I use? Who should I talk to?
>
> Kerry

C

5. Case study AC 1.1, 2.1, 2.2

> Sara was worried because she had had sex with her boyfriend. They had not used anything. She went to the sexual health clinic. She was pleased because she did not need an appointment. The nurse was nice. She did a pregnancy test. Sara was not pregnant. The nurse told Sara that she was a lucky girl. The nurse talked to Sara. She gave her free condoms and showed her how to use them. She also gave Sara the pill to take each day.

1. Where did Sara go and who did she see?
2. Why did the nurse say that Sara was a lucky girl?
3. What methods is Sara using now?

Stages of pregnancy

Most pregnancies last for 9 months or around 40 weeks. On these pages we look at what happens between conception and birth.

Say again?

Conception – the point at which the sperm from the father meets the egg from the mother – this is when the baby is made

egg at hour 1

blastocyst at week 1

foetus at week 5

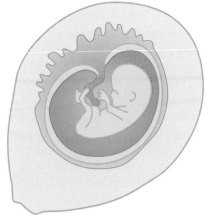

foetus at 12 weeks

Stage 1: The first 12 weeks

When a man's sperm enters a woman's egg, a baby is on the way to being made. Look at how the egg grows by making new cells.

The egg also moves in the first week and finds a home in the side of the womb. Here a placenta will develop. Its job is to feed the baby and keep it alive. The baby is joined to the placenta by a cord. This is called the umbilical cord. The baby will grow inside a special sac. The sac fills with liquid called amniotic fluid. This will help keep it safe. By week 12, the baby is formed although it is very small. It is called a foetus.

Spot it
Can you spot how much the baby grows in the first 12 weeks?

Stage 2: 13–28 weeks

In this stage, the baby gets bigger. It also gets stronger. The baby can move around inside the amniotic sac. The umbilical cord keeps on passing everything the baby needs from the placenta. By week 24 the baby can suck its thumb.

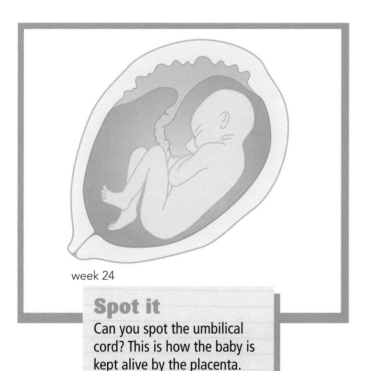

week 24

Spot it
Can you spot the umbilical cord? This is how the baby is kept alive by the placenta.

Stage 3: 28–40 weeks

In this stage, the baby is getting bigger day by day. It will also be getting stronger. This is important as when the baby is born it will need to breathe by itself and suck. Most babies are born at 40 weeks. This is called 'term'. The mother will feel the muscles around her stomach tighten. These are called contractions. They help to push the baby out. The baby will come out head first. Then the baby's body will come out. Once the baby is safely born, the umbilical cord is cut. The baby can now survive alone.

Pregnancy words — **High five**

1. Conception – when the sperm meets the egg.
2. Placenta – this keeps the baby alive.
3. Umbilical cord – this is the link between the baby and the placenta.
4. Amniotic sac – this is the bag in which the baby lives. It is filled with fluid.
5. Foetus – this is what doctors call an unborn baby.

Care required for a mum-to-be

Pregnant women have to take care of themselves. They also need to take care of their unborn baby. On these pages we will look at ways to do this.

Let's start with the mum-to-be! There are many ways that pregnant women can look after themselves.

Going to the doctor

The doctor needs to know that a woman is having a baby. The doctor will sort lots of things out. The doctor will contact the hospital. The doctor will contact a **midwife**.

Say again?

Midwife – this is a person trained to look after mums-to-be and to help them give birth

Going to check ups

When women are pregnant they will see the midwife. She will check that they are well. She will check that the baby is well. Some checks may be done at the doctor's. Some checks may be done at the hospital. These checks are known as **antenatal** checks.

Say again?

Antenatal – this means the time before a baby is born

See it, think it

The midwife is checking the baby by doing a scan. Why is it important to go to antenatal check ups?

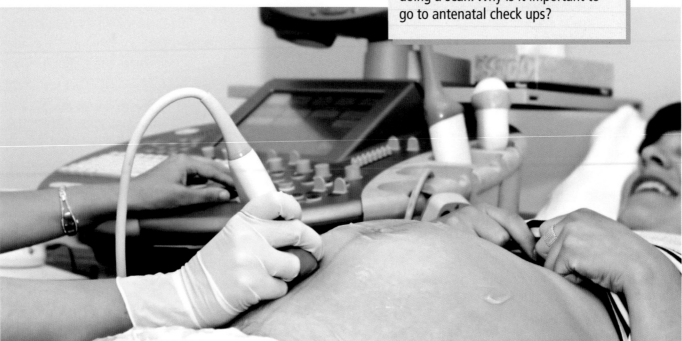

Eating healthy food

For the baby to be healthy, the mum has to eat healthy food. She does not have to eat more food. But she does have to eat plenty of fruit and vegetables. You can read more about healthy food.

 Look at pages 44–46 and page 48 for more information.

Giving up smoking

Pregnant women should give up smoking. It is not good for the woman. It is not good for her baby.

Not drinking alcohol

Alcohol is not good for pregnant women. It is not good for the baby.

Not taking drugs

Pregnant women should not take any drugs. Even drugs that you can buy at the chemist's can hurt an unborn baby.

Factors that can harm an unborn baby

There are several things that can harm a baby before it is born. The table below shows what can happen if a mum-to-be does any of these things.

Factor	Before birth	When born
✗ Smoking when pregnant	• can stop the baby from growing strong • can cause the baby to have problems breathing	• smoking is linked to cot death (when babies die while they are sleeping)
✗ Drinking alcohol when pregnant	• can stop the baby from growing properly	• can make it hard for the baby to learn
✗ Taking drugs when pregnant	• can kill the baby • can stop the baby from growing properly	• can make the baby poorly • can make it hard for the baby to learn
✗ Having a bad diet when pregnant	• can stop the baby from growing well • can make birth more difficult	• can make the baby poorly

Support for new parents

The first few weeks after a baby is born are hard for parents. They have to make changes to their lives. They have to feed the baby in the day and at night.

Let's look at what support parents may need.

Advice about the baby

New parents have to learn how to feed and care for a baby. They have to learn what to do if the baby cries a lot. They also need to know how to keep the baby healthy.

Help for the mother

Giving birth is tiring. It takes a while for the body to get back to normal. Sometimes mothers can get infections.

Some mothers also get depressed. This is called **post-natal** depression. It can become quite serious.

Say again?

Post-natal – this is about what happens after the baby is born

See it, think it

Midwives come in every day to start with. Why does this help new parents?

Help for the parents

Parents have to learn new skills. They have to change their lives. This can cause problems between them. They may have arguments.

Some parents also need help finding somewhere to live. Some parents may also have money problems.

Support for parents

There are many places where parents can get help.

About the baby

For the first few days, a midwife will come and help parents. The midwife will check the baby and the mother. The midwife will also give advice.

Afterwards parents can see their health visitor. Some health visitors will come to the house. Parents can also go to health clinics. Midwives and health visitors can talk to parents about caring for the baby.

Help for the mother

If the mother does not feel well, she can go to the doctor. She can also tell the midwife or the health visitor. The health visitor will also keep an eye on her, as many mothers get depressed. The good news is that the depression can be treated.

Help for parents

When parents have problems with each other, they can get counselling. They can also talk to other parents on the Internet. Sharing problems can often help. Families might also help parents by offering to take the baby for a while.

Find out!

Find out the phone number of your local Relate service. This is the service that helps couples who have problems in their relationship.

The local Citizens' Advice Bureau (CAB) helps parents who have problems with money or with finding somewhere to live. They give free advice.

Support for parents **High five**

1. New parents have to learn new skills to care for their baby.
2. Midwives come in at first to help parents.
3. Health visitors can give parents advice.
4. The Citizens' Advice Bureau can give advice about money and housing.
5. Relate is an organisation that helps couples with their relationships.

Activity centre 20

I. Match up   AC I.I

Can you match up the pictures to the following stages?

Conception	18 weeks
10 days	38 weeks

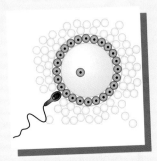 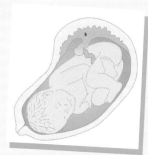  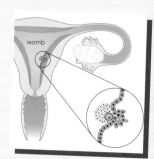

2. Remember me?   AC I.I

Can you remember the three stages of pregnancy? Fill in the spaces in this chart.

Stage	Weeks	What happens
Stage I	0–12	
	13–28	The baby is getting bigger. It can suck its thumb at 24 weeks.
Stage 3	28–40	The baby is getting bigger. At around 40 weeks, the mother will give birth. The umbilical cord is cut.

3. True or false? AC 2.1

Which of these statements are true and which are false?

	True	False
Mums-to-be should see their doctor	☐	☐
Mums-to-be should watch television	☐	☐
Mums-to-be should eat fruit and vegetables	☐	☐
Mums-to-be should smoke more	☐	☐

5. Match up AC 3.1, 3.2

Can you work out where people can get support? Match the problem with the correct source of support.

Problem	Support
Baby is not feeding	Relate counsellor
Mum is still bleeding	Doctor
Parents are arguing	Midwife or health visitor

4. Odd one out! AC 2.2

All but one of these actions could harm a baby. Which is the odd one out?

If mum smokes

If mum takes drugs

If mum eats cabbage

If mum drinks cider

6. Agony page AC 3.2

Tell this mother where she can get help.

My baby is 4 weeks old. She keeps crying. I can't make her stop. It makes me cry. I get angry as well.

Anya

7. Do it! AC 3.2

Find out where your local health clinic is.

10

Personal development

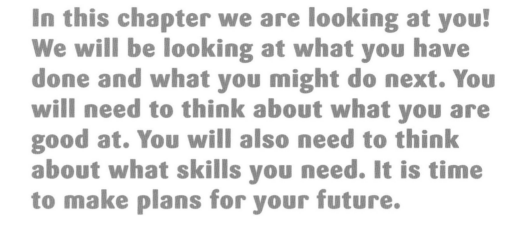

In this chapter we are looking at you! We will be looking at what you have done and what you might do next. You will need to think about what you are good at. You will also need to think about what skills you need. It is time to make plans for your future.

The units covered in this chapter are:

CFC19 Self development
CFC16 Preparing for your next steps

In this chapter you will learn about:

- how to describe your achievements and interests and how these have contributed to your development and current situation
- your strengths in relation to skills, qualities and abilities, and assess their importance for the future
- areas for further development, why they need to be developed and how
- how to match your skills, qualities and abilities to the requirements of education or a career
- your learning style and how your career and education choices may be influenced by this
- how to identify a range of personal goals and produce an action plan
- how to investigate potential career goals
- the steps needed to achieve personal goals and identify barriers
- sources of information for training or employment
- training and employment opportunities
- writing about personal information and skills for application forms or CVs
- skills and knowledge required for particular career paths
- the steps to recruitment and the importance of personal preparation for interview.

Your achievements and interests matter

Everyone has something that they can do. This is called an achievement. Achievements can be quite small. You need to think about your achievements.

Here are some examples of **achievements**.

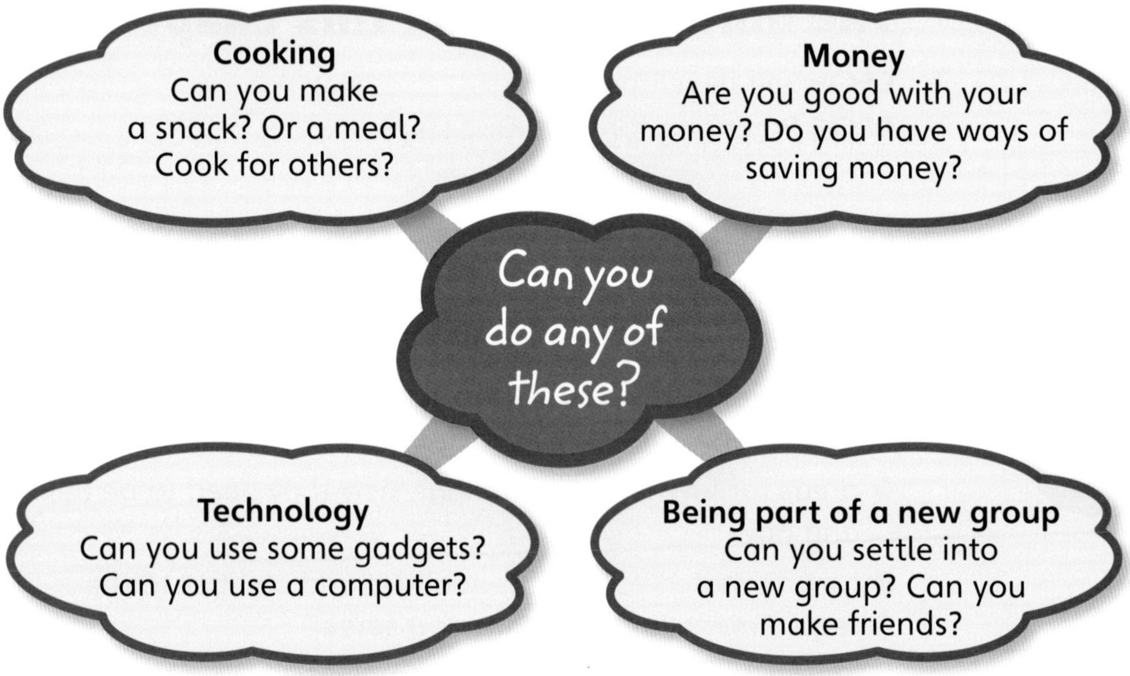

Cooking
Can you make
a snack? Or a meal?
Cook for others?

Money
Are you good with your
money? Do you have ways of
saving money?

*Can you
do any of
these?*

Technology
Can you use some gadgets?
Can you use a computer?

Being part of a new group
Can you settle into
a new group? Can you
make friends?

Say again?

Achievement – something that you have learned how to do

Thinking about your achievements

You need to think about two things you have achieved. Think about what you had to do for each achievement. Here are some questions.

- When did you do it?
- How long did it take?
- Who helped you?
- Why did you do it?
- What did you learn?
- What skills were needed?

Interests

Everyone has things that they like doing. These are called interests. You need to think about two interests that you have. Let's look at some examples.

Sports and keeping fit
Do you play any sports? Do you walk or take exercise?

Games
Do you enjoy playing board games? Do you enjoy computer or video games?

Do you do any of these?

Making or listening to music
Are you in a band? Do you play an instrument? Do you like listening to music?

Pets
Do you have any pets? Do you look after them?

Why your achievements and interests matter

Every new skill and every new interest changes us. We might meet new people. We might gain in confidence. For this unit, you need to think about how your achievements and interests have made a difference to you. Let's look at the speech bubbles to see some of the things that people say.

I have learned to ask for help when I don't understand.

I am more patient.

I am not afraid of trying something new.

I have learned that you have to give things time.

I have learned how to make new friends.

Your strengths

For this unit, you have to think about your skills, qualities and abilities. You also have to work out how they might help you.

Let's look at some examples of **skills**, **qualities** and **abilities**.

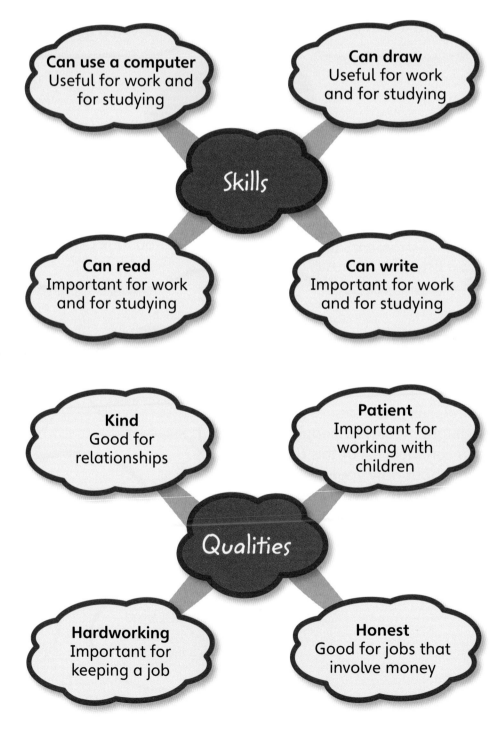

Can use a computer
Useful for work and for studying

Can draw
Useful for work and for studying

Skills

Can read
Important for work and for studying

Can write
Important for work and for studying

Kind
Good for relationships

Patient
Important for working with children

Qualities

Hardworking
Important for keeping a job

Honest
Good for jobs that involve money

Good at listening
Good for work and social relationships

Good with children
Good for working with children

Abilities

Can learn things quickly
Useful if doing something new

Can get on with people
Good if part of a team or in a new group

Say again?

Skills – things that you have learned to do, like using a computer
Qualities – good things about you as a person, such as being honest
Abilities – things that you seem naturally good at doing, like singing

Over to you...

Start thinking about your skills, qualities and abilities.

See it, think it

These people have thought about what they need to do. What areas do you need to work on?

Areas for improvement

No one is perfect. For this unit, you need to think about areas that you could work on. Let's look at some examples.

I need to work on my spelling so that I can get a job. I will need to ask for help from my tutor.

Dan

I need to stop messing around. This will help me get a job with children. I am going to sit away from my friends in class.

Sam

I need to try harder. This will help me with my studying. I will do my work first before turning on the computer.

Jo

How to use your strengths

For this unit, you will need to think about what you might do next. Thinking about your strengths will help you. This is because you should try and do something that builds on your strengths.

Let's look at what strengths are needed to work with children and why.

Reading and writing	Being reliable and hardworking.
Being ready to listen	Good communication skills

↓ ↓

These strengths are needed in order to study. Studying will help you learn more about children.	You need experience to get a job with children. You will need experience as part of the qualification.

↓ ↓

Qualification	Experience

↓ ↓

Working with children

Spot it
Can you spot how this nursery worker is good at communicating?

Your learning style

Your next step will probably mean learning new skills. For this unit, you need to think about how you learn best. Let's look at some examples of ways in which people find it easy or hard to learn.

See it, think it
Can you think of any other skills, qualities or abilities that someone might need to work with children?

In a group or by yourself?

Some people find it better to learn in small groups or by themselves. Others like to be with other people.

Quiet or loud?

Some people like having music on while they work or are happy when it is noisy. Others like it to be quiet.

Deadline or no pressure?

Some people like being told when things have to be finished. Others like to work at their own pace.

Listening or doing?

Some people like to learn by listening. Others like to learn by doing.

Praise or self-motivated?

Some people need praise or rewards. They find it hard if no one is noticing what they are doing.

Day or night?

Some people find it hard to get up in the morning to study. Others find it hard to go to an evening class.

Your learning style and what you do next

Knowing your learning style will help you decide what to do next. If you find it best to work in a group, you might like to do a course in a college. If you find it best to work in the evening, you might look for an evening class.

Over to you...

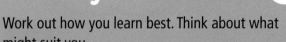

Work out how you learn best. Think about what might suit you.

Personal goals

It is good to have some personal goals. Personal goals might help us to build on our strengths. Some goals might help us with our weaknesses.

Choosing personal goals

It is a good idea to choose goals that are important to you. You need to base goals on what is possible in the area you live in.

You may want to look back at page 205 at the areas for improvement that you chose.

Let's look at the four personal goals that Dan has set himself.

Visit a school
To find out more about working in a school

Sign up for a child development course
To get qualified to work in a school

Dan's personal goals

Get help with reading and writing
To help with the course

Learn how to use the computer
To help with the course

What Dan says about his goals

Dan

> I chose these goals because I want to work in a school. I think that I am good with children. I need a qualification and there is a college in my area. I need to spell and write to do the qualification so I am going to get some help. I thought it would be good to visit a school before starting. I also thought it would be good to learn to use the computer so I can do my work on it.

Over to you...

Working out your personal goals needs some time and thought. Let's look at the steps involved.

1. What can I do now?
2. What do I need to improve?
3. What do I know about my learning style?
4. What do I want to do?
5. What goals will help me to get this type of work?
6. What is available where I live?

Think about four personal goals that you could set. If you want to work with children, look back at page 206 to see what skills are needed. You will need to find out what is possible in your area. If you are not sure what to do, one of your goals might be to see a **careers advisor**.

Say again?

Careers advisor – someone who helps you think about what work you might do

Action plans

For this part of the unit, you need to draw up an action plan. You will need to show how you will work towards the goals that you thought about on page 209.

Say again?

Action plan – a detailed plan of what you want to do and how to do it

SMART plans

For a plan to work, they need to be carefully thought out. 'SMART' is often used when people draw up plans. Let's look at what it means.

S = Specific

This means thinking carefully about what you want to do. You will probably need to break things down into tiny steps.

✔ I will learn how to log onto the Internet.

✗ I will learn how to be good with computers.

M = Measurable

This is about deciding how you can show that you reached the task.

✔ I will be able to log onto the Internet without any help.

✗ I will just know that I can do it.

A = Achievable and
R = Realistic

This is about making sure that what you are aiming to do is possible.

✔ I know that there is a computer that I can use. A friend says that she will show me.

✗ There is no one who can show me how to use the computer. I might learn how to do it from a book.

T = Timed

This is about making it clear when you will complete the step or goal.

✔ I will set a target of a week to do it.

✗ It will just happen!

Tiny steps

When you set goals for yourself, you have to break everything down into tiny steps. This way you are more likely to get there. It is a little like taking a journey. Let's look at ten of the steps Dan took in order to use a computer. It took him several weeks. For each step, Dan set himself a time limit. This way he kept on going.

Steps to find out how to use the computer:

1. Work out where there are classes or a friend to help me.
2. Learn how to turn the computer on and off.
3. Find my way around the keyboard.
4. Learn how to create a desktop.
5. Learn how to log onto the Internet.
6. Learn how to do a search.
7. Learn how to create a folder.
8. Learn how to save files.
9. Learn how to type a simple letter.
10. Learn how to cut and paste.

Dan

See it, think it

Why do you think Dan has broken his goal into small steps? How will this help him?

Goals	Steps to reach my goal	Timescale for my actions	Review of my progress	When I expect to reach my goal
To learn to use the computer	• Work out where there are classes or a friend to help me • Learn how to turn the computer on and off • Find my way around the keyboard	23/6/11 1/7/11 15/7/11	I will meet with my teacher every two weeks. I will show what I can do.	Six months

Activity centre 21

1. Do it!   AC 1.1

Talk about two achievements. Talk about what they were. Talk about what you had to do.

2. Do it!   AC 2.2

Make a list of the skills, qualities and abilities that you would like to develop. Why are they important?

3. Do it!   AC 2.2

See if you can fill in this table.

Areas for improvement	Why you need to improve	How you might do this
Getting into college on time.	I need to show an employer that I am reliable.	Will go to bed half an hour earlier. Will get an earlier bus.

4. Agony page   AC 3.1

What sort of job could Matt get with these skills, qualities and abilities?

> I can drive. I can also use a computer. I think that I get on with people. I am not sure how these can help me. Have you any ideas?
>
> Matt

5. Do it!   AC 2.3

Find out what skills, qualities and abilities are needed for the work that you would like to do next. Find out if you need to take a qualification.

6. Do it! AC 4.1

Make a list of your personal goals. Think about what you would really like to achieve. Remember that these can be long-term goals.

8. Do it! AC 1.1

Make a poster that shows other people your interests.

9. Case study AC 4.2, 5.1

Rebecca wants to work in a nursery. She knows she will need to get a qualification. She does not like writing. She knows that this is because she is so slow. She is good with children and she is not afraid of hard work. Rebecca visited a local nursery. They have said that they will consider her if she can do her training.

1. Why should Rebecca make working in a nursery her personal goal?

2. Think of some steps that could go on Rebecca's action plan to help her.

7. Agony page AC 3.1

Tell Mandy why her way of learning might not fit this way of getting a qualification.

I like learning in a group. I also learn best when I have deadlines. I fall asleep late in the day. I also get nervous when people watch me. My mum says that I could work in a nursery and get a qualification at the same time. I would only have to go to college one evening a week. There are no exams. Someone would watch me work instead. I am not sure. What do you think?

Mandy

10. Do it! AC 5.1

Before drawing up your action plan, find out about the job and training opportunities that are available in your area.

Personal career goals

It is useful to think about what you might like to do next. In this unit, you will need to think about what you could do next and how you could go about it.

Let's begin by thinking about your possible career goals.

What do you like doing?

A good starting point is to think about what type of work you enjoy doing. On this course, we have been looking at children. Begin by thinking if you have enjoyed learning about children.

Possible careers working with children

There are many careers where you can work with children. Here are some examples. Some of the jobs shown below will need you to train for a number of years.

Working in a school	Teacher Teaching assistant Midday supervisor Special needs assistant
Working in a pre-school	Pre-school leader Pre-school worker Special needs co-ordinator (SENCO)
Working in a nursery	Manager Nursery nurse Special needs co-ordinator (SENCO)
Working in a home setting	Childminder Nanny
Working in an afterschool club/holiday club	Manager Playworker
Working with older children	Playworker Youth worker

Your next steps

Your next step will be to find out more about your career choice. Once you have done this, you will know what training, skills and experience you need. Below are some examples of some next steps.

Dan: I want to help children with special needs. I need to work on my reading and writing.

Jo: I want to be a nanny. I need to go back to college to get another qualification.

Sam: I want to work in a pre-school. I need to improve my English

Janet: I want to be a midday supervisor. I need to do a food hygiene course.

Barriers

It is important to think about what might stop you from achieving your career goal. You also need to think about how you can overcome these. Let's look at a few possible **barriers**.

Say again?

Barrier – something that might stop you from doing what you want

'I have a baby to look after. I cannot go to college.'

'I need to earn money while I am learning.'

'I am scared that everyone will laugh at me.'

'I don't like trying out new things.'

See it, think it
How might the barriers described in the speech bubbles get in the way?

Common barriers   High five
1. Time
2. Money
3. Confidence
4. Travelling distance
5. Motivation

Opportunities for training and work

Once you have begun to think about your career goal, you need to get more advice. Let's look at some of the places you can go to get more information.

Job Centre	Every town has a job centre. You can find out what jobs there are and get advice.
Tutor/Teacher	Your tutor and teacher will be able to tell you about training opportunities. They may give you advice about your career.
Careers advisors	These are people who give advice and information about careers. You may find them in your school or college.
Connexions advisors	Connexions is an advice service for young people. You can talk to an advisor on the phone or go to a centre.
Websites	There are some websites for young people and adults that give information about training and career advice.

Training opportunities

For many careers, you may need more training. To find out more about training opportunities in your area, you can visit your local college or careers advisor. Let's look at some examples of training opportunities.

Short courses

Short courses may be over a day or a week. Short courses often give you particular knowledge or skills. Examples of short courses include First Aid, Food Hygiene and Manual Handling.

Apprenticeships

It is possible to work with children and train at the same time. You would learn on the job and also study at home. Apprenticeships work well if you are a hard worker. You have to study hard as well as work hard.

Part time

If you need money, you might find a job and study part time or in the evenings. It might take you longer to get your qualification this way.

 To obtain a secure link to a website which offers information about training and career advice, see the Websites section on page ii.

Full time

Some courses are full time. You would probably study in a group at college. As part of your course, you may go on work experience.

Distance learning

Distance learning is learning mainly at home. You might be given things to do each week or month. Most distance learning courses are done through the Internet. You send work in and get information via the Internet. Distance learning works well if you are very motivated and good at working alone.

Employment options

Your employment options will depend on your qualifications so far and your work experience. Your attitude and how hard you work will also be important.

Some employment options

High five

1. Babysitting
2. Mother's help/au pair
3. Midday supervisor at a school
4. Volunteer/trainee at a local playgroup
5. Volunteer/trainee in a nursery

Guess what!

Volunteering can be a good way of getting a training place as well as work experience.

Personal skills

In order to apply for a job or a training place, you need to work out what your skills are. This will help you to work out what type of jobs you should be looking for.

Let's look at some of the personal skills that you might have. You may have gained some of these by doing this course.

Working with children

Think about what you have learned about working with children. Look back at some of the units that you have completed for this course. Make a list of what you might have learned. Opposite are some of the things that you might be able to do.

- Choose a story for a young child.
- Find hazards in the home.
- Plan a healthy meal for a young child.
- Think of musical activities for a young child.

Personal qualities

You need to think about your personal qualities. These are very important when thinking about what you want to do. Go back to page 204 to look at examples of these. Opposite are some examples of personal qualities.

Spot it
What skills has this student got?

Say again?

Persistent – this is about being able to keep on trying and not giving up

Communication skills

You might like to think about your communication skills. Think about which of these you can do.

- Talk and listen to adults.
- Talk and listen to babies.
- Talk and listen to young children.
- Stand up and present information.

- Make notes.
- Use a telephone.
- Write things down.
- Read and understand information.

See it, think it
What skills does a sales person need?

Interpersonal skills

You need to think about how well you get on with people. Here are some questions to think about.

- Do you like being by yourself?
- Do you work well in a team?
- Do you prefer to work in a small group or pairs?
- How easy do you find meeting new people?

Say again?

Interpersonal skills – these are about how you get on with people

Application forms and CVs

When you apply for a job or training place, you need to give information about yourself. You may be asked to do this by filling in an application form or sending a CV.

Let's look at the type of information that you might need to put on an **application form** or a **CV**.

Name

You will always need to put your full name. Do not put your nickname.

Address

Give an address where letters can be sent to. You should include the postcode.

Phone number

Put the best number for someone to ring you. If it is not your own phone, you should put this in brackets, for example: 01346 228771 (work number).

Curriculum Vitae

Dan Baker
84 Hurst St, James Town, GH3 1FD
0776 431 346
Born: 19.01.1995

Education

| 2010-present | James Town College I am studying childcare |
| 2005-2010 | James Town School |

Work experience

2009-present   **Newsagents Saturday job**
I work at the till and stacking shelves in Hurst Street Newsagents on Saturdays.

2010-present   **Under 7s football coaching**
On Sundays I help out with football coaching of my local under 7s team.

2011-present   **Baby sitting**
I baby sit for my aunt's children on a regular basis. Her children are 7 and 10 years old.

References
Paul Clark, 11 Coniston Road, Coopertown, BN4 6JY

Spot it
Can you spot some personal information on this CV?

Say again?

Application form – this is a form that you fill in – it asks questions about what you have done and learned

CV – this is all about you and is a document that you write – it shows what you have done and learned

Education

You will need to write about what courses you have taken. If you have any qualifications you need to write down what they are. You must also put the dates and any grades. You might also need to put down the secondary school or college that you went to.

Previous employment/ work experience

You should write about any job or work experience you have had. Think about what skills you needed. Write about what you have learned. You should always write the dates you worked there.

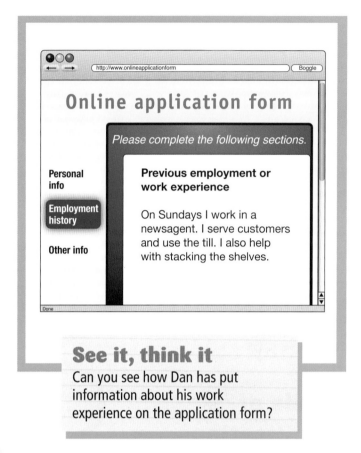

Online application form

Please complete the following sections.

Personal info

Employment history

Other info

Previous employment or work experience

On Sundays I work in a newsagent. I serve customers and use the till. I also help with stacking the shelves.

See it, think it
Can you see how Dan has put information about his work experience on the application form?

Say again?

Previous employment – this is about paid work that you have had before

Hobbies and interests

Think about what you do if you have spare time. Do not put down things that might not look good!

References

You need to think of two people that can tell someone what your good qualities are. They cannot be family members. These people will give you a reference and are known as referees. Think about teachers, tutors and people who have worked with you. Before writing their names down, you must ask them first. You must also write down their address and either a phone number or an email address for them.

Skills and knowledge

Every job needs you to have some skills and knowledge. For some training places, you may need some skills and knowledge too.

For this unit, you need to show that you have thought about the skills you already have, but also the skills and knowledge needed for your next steps.

Back on page 214 we looked at some career options. Let's look now at some of the skills that you might need for these jobs.

Levels of qualifications

A qualification shows that you have knowledge and skills. Qualifications are at different levels. The course that you are doing is at level 1. Some jobs need you to have a level 2 qualification. For jobs where you work alone with children, a level 3 qualification is needed.

Teaching assistant

If you want to be a teaching assistant, you would need to show that you can work well with children. You may also need a childcare or teaching assistant qualification at level 2 or 3.

Skills for working with children

- Patience
- Reliable and hardworking
- Able to keep environment clean, tidy and attractive
- Able to make children feel relaxed and happy
- Able to communicate with parents and children
- Able to plan for children
- Able to observe children
- Able to work in a team

See it, think it
Can you think of other skills that might be needed if you worked with a baby?

Special needs assistant

If you want to be a special needs assistant, you would need to show that you can work well with children. You may also need to have a childcare or teaching assistant qualification at level 2 or 3.

Midday supervisor

If you want to be a midday supervisor in a school, you would need to show that you can work well with children. You would also need to show that you have good food hygiene skills. You might also need to learn about first aid.

Childminder

If you want to work as a childminder, you would need to work well with children. You should also have a qualification at level 3 because you would work alone with children.

Nursery assistant/work in a pre-school

If you want to be a nursery assistant, you would need to show that you can work well with young children. You would also need a childcare qualification at level 2.

Nursery nurse in a school

If you want to work as a nursery nurse in a school, you would need to show that you can work well with young children. You would also need a childcare qualification at level 3.

Nanny

If you want to work as a nanny, you would need to show that you can work well with young children. You should also have a qualification at level 3 because you would work alone with children.

Playworker

If you want to work as a playworker in an after-school club or during the holidays, you would need to show that you can work with children in a play setting. You might also need a qualification in playwork or childcare at level 2 or 3.

See it, think it
This childminder looks after children in her own home. Why does she need a level 3 qualification?

Steps to recruitment

In order to get a job or a training place, there are a few steps to take first. Let's look at them.

Finding a job or training place

If you are looking for a job, try the job centre, local newspaper or the Internet.

If you are looking for a training place, try the local college, careers service or job centre.

Contacting the employer or training provider

Once you have found a job or training place, you need to contact the employer or training provider. They may send you an information pack or more details. Sometimes you may be asked to go in and collect information.

Applying for the job or training place

Once you have found out about the job or training place, you need to apply. Sometimes there is a form to fill in. This is called an application form. Sometimes you might be asked to send in your CV. Sometimes, you have to phone in to say that you are interested. It is important to follow carefully the instructions you have been given, so do not send in your CV if there is an application form. You should also get your application in on time.

Invitation to an interview

If the employer or training provider likes your application, they may invite you for an interview. They may write you a letter or phone you. You must let them know that you can come to the interview. Remember to write down the date and time.

Interview

On the day of the interview, you may need to take some information with you. You must also prepare for the interview. This will help you to do well. (Look at pages 226–227 to see how to prepare.)

Confirmation

If you have done well at interview, you may be told that you have got the job or training place. Sometimes you will have to wait for a letter or phone call. Remember to thank the person.

Application form

Please complete the following sections.

Name:	Chioma Willis
Address:	23 Cross St, Weston-Upon-Reed, HD3 1JH
Telephone number:	0791 453 211

Previous employment or work experience

> I work as a waitress in a café. I take orders and serve customers. I also make teas and coffees.

See it, think it
Why is it important to fill in the application form neatly?

Feedback

If you have not been offered the job or training place, it is a good idea to find out why. This means asking for feedback. It can be hard to have **feedback** that is not good. But it can help you to be better for the next time.

Say again?

Apply for a job/training place – this is about showing that you want the job or training place – you might have to fill in a form or send in your CV
Feedback – comments about how you have done

Preparation for interview

Getting ready for an interview is important. People who get ready for interview are likely to get the job or the training place.

Let's look at why preparation makes the difference.

I think that I am doing well. Wearing these clothes means I feel that I fit in here. I am less nervous than usual. I can answer most of the questions.

I can see that he has made an effort. He was on time. His answers are good. He knows quite a lot about what we do. He seems like he really wants this job.

See it, think it
Dan has prepared for his job interview. How is it helping him?

Ways of preparing for an interview

Most people find interviews difficult. Some people get nervous. Some people find it hard to talk in front of a stranger. Others find that they talk too much. There are some simple ways to prepare for an interview. Let's look at a few.

Preparing for interview   High five

1. Read about the job or course.
2. Find out where you have to go.
3. Decide what you will wear.
4. Work out what you need to take, e.g. certificates and references.
5. Ask someone to give you a practice interview.

What you can do	Why
Work out where you have to go before the day.	To get there on time
Work out what you should wear.	To look right for the job or course
Find out about the job or course.	To show that you are interested
Put any certificates or other information together.	To show the interviewer that you are organised
Think about what questions might come up.	To practise answers

Practising for an interview

It can be a good idea to practise for an interview. Ask a friend or someone you trust to ask you a few questions. Tell them about what type of work or training you are hoping to do. It may seem strange, but practising your answers aloud can really help. It can help you to feel more confident.

Common interview questions   High five

1. Tell me about yourself.
2. Why are you interested in this job?
3. What are your strengths?
4. What are your weaknesses?
5. Where do you see yourself in 3 years from now?

Activity centre 22

1. Agony page
AC 1.1, 1.2, 1.3

Think of something you could tell Sandeesh to help her decide what to do.

> I am not sure what to do with my life. I am 16 years old. I like working with children, but I have not got any qualifications. I have done some babysitting. I think it might be good to work with children in a home setting. Any suggestions?
>
> Sandeesh

2. Odd one out!
AC 2.1

All but one of these could give you information about training or employment. Which is the odd one out?

Job centre

Call centre

Careers advisor

Connexions advisor

3. Do it!
AC 2.2, 2.3

Make a list of training and employment options that you might have.

4. Match up
AC 2.3

Match up the job titles with the sentences below.

**Special needs assistant   Playworker
Midday supervisor   Pre-school worker**

I work with children in a local playgroup.

I work with children in an after-school club.

I work with children who need extra support to learn.

I work with children at lunch times.

5. Do it!
AC 3.1

Working with a friend or someone who knows you well, make a list of skills that you have.

6. Do it! AC 3.2

Look at some different CVs and application forms. What type of information is needed?

7. Do it! AC 2.3, 3.3

Make a poster that shows some of the different career options for working with children. For each option, put the qualification level that might be needed.

8. Odd one out! AC 3.3

All but one of these are skills for working with children. Which is the odd one out?

Communication skills
Drawing and painting skills
Patience and reliability
Knowledge about child development

9. Do it! AC 4.I

Make a poster that shows the steps you need to take to get a job.

10. Case study AC 4.I

C

Dan is fed up. He wanted to get a job working in a school. He got an interview. But he did not get the job. After a couple of days, he sent an email to the school. He asked for feedback on his application. The headteacher sent him an email later. Dan learned about why he did not get the job. He found out that during the interview, he did not look at the headteacher. He also found out that he did not have enough experience.

I. Why did Dan need feedback?
2. How did the feedback help Dan?
3. Why might Dan get a job next time?

II. Agony page AC 4.2

Tell Jo why preparing for interview is important. Give her some ideas of what she could do.

I have an interview next week. If I do well, I can get a training place. My mum says that I should prepare for it. But I can't see the point. I don't know how I would prepare.

Jo

Index